The Naxal Threat:
Causes, State Responses and Consequences

The Naxal Threat:
Causes, State Responses and Consequences

Editor

V.R. Raghavan

Published for
Centre for Security Analysis
Chennai, India

Vij Books India Pvt Ltd
New Delhi, India

Published by

Vij Books India Pvt Ltd

2/19, Ansari Road, Darya Ganj
New Delhi - 110002
Phones: 91-11-65449971, 91-11- 43596460
Fax: 91-11-47340674
e-mail : vijbooks@rediffmail.com
web : www.vijbooks.com

Centre for Security Analysis

"9-B" Ninth Floor,
Chesney Nilgiri, 71, Ethiraj Salai,
Egmore, Chennai-600008
Tamil Nadu, India
+91-44-65291889
office@csa-chennai.org
www.csa-chennai.org

First Published : 2011

ISBN 13 : 978-93-80177-77-9

Acknowledgement

The Centre for Security Analysis (CSA) has undertaken a three year research project **Internal Conflicts and Transnational Consequences** supported by the John D and Catherine T MacArthur Foundation. This volume is part of the ongoing project and its publication has been possible by the project grant.

TABLE OF CONTENTS

FOREWORD

Conflicts have for long been studied to find ways for governments to resolve them. While the causes of a conflict, if not addressed can push the conflict into an upward spiral, equal attention needs to be directed to the consequences from the conflict. In protracted conflicts, their consequences in themselves turn into causes. They generate vested interests in sustaining the conflict. They also create new stakeholders other than those directly involved in the conflict. Overtime, consequences tend to drive and sustain the conflict and become a motivating factor in sustaining the conflict. Hence studying the consequences of the conflict can provide new insight for policy formulations and strategies for conflict resolution.

This understanding forms the basis of CSA's MacArthur Foundation funded project on *Internal Conflicts and Transnational Consequences*. The project studies conflicts in India, Sri Lanka, Nepal and Myanmar and this book forms a part of the study.

The cluster of the four conflicts zones, forming part of this project, is a unique case study of almost similar internal conflicts with different causes within varied governance systems. A full fledged democracy with all its challenges in India, a monarchy and now transitional democracy in Nepal, military dictatorship in Myanmar and presidential form of democracy with high developmental index in Sri Lanka provide for unique but overlapping types of systems and conflicts. In Nepal, a monarchy led social order was part of the problem and still continues to be behind the scene. In Sri Lanka, democratically elected governments with a certain national vision preferred to rule with a divisive strategy focused in favour of majority community. Myanmar witnessed a military junta working against both the pro-democracy entities and ethnic minority groups. While these countries have dealt with their conflicts in different ways there are also similarities and this study draws on these similarities in order to streamline policy analysis and the state's responses.

At this point CSA has conducted major conferences on Myanmar, Nepal, India's Northeast, Jammu and Kashmir and Sri Lanka. The conference on Myanmar, held in Singapore, provided an insight into how the conflict in Myanmar has created vested interests, among other consequences, in Thailand and other parts of the world. The conference on Nepal, held in Varanasi, brought together not only scholars and Nepalese nationals but also representatives from the villages in border States of Uttar Pradesh and Bihar. It is not only the Maoists who matter but also these villagers who in a way provide the sustenance. The links with this region go up to narcotics and smuggling as well.

The conferences on Jammu and Kashmir held in Jammu and on India's Northeast held in Delhi also brought together participants who work from the affected regions as well as others who are part of the conflict society. Similarly, the conference on Sri Lanka, held in Colombo, brought together the key actors involved in the peace process, scholars as well as observers who analyzed the conflict in the light of its consequences.

This volume is about the Naxal Threat in India, its causes, state responses and consequences. Naxalism existed in some form or the other for more than sixty years. The respective states were able to resolve it. The year 2004, however, was a turning point in the history of Naxalism when the Peoples' War group (PWG) and the Maoist Communist Centre (MCC) merged to form the Communist party of India (Maoist). Thereafter, Naxal movement transformed from a mere social movement fighting for the rights of the poor and landless to a multi dimensional movement seeking to overthrow democratic governance in India and replace it with a more equitable and egalitarian new order. There has been a paradigm shift in ideology, organization and strategy of Naxals which has brought in greater organizational cohesion and more concerted action with an objective of establishing the Red Corridor from North Bihar to the underdeveloped hinterland of Jharkhand, Orissa, Chhattisgarh, Andhra Pradesh, Maharashtra and Karnataka. The recent surge in Naxal violence has established beyond doubt that it is much more than a mere law and order problem. It is believed that Naxalism has affected 35 percent of the population and operate in a vacuum created by failure of administrative and political institutions, espouse local demands and take advantage of the prevalent alienation and injustice among the exploited sections of the population and seek to offer an alternative system of governance which promises emancipation of these sections from the clutches of exploiter classes through the barrel of the gun. The challenges faced by the government are also multidimensional as it is very complex socio- politico- economic problem combined with armed violence. Now that increasing evidence is being found of their linkages with the forces hostile to the interests of our country, there is definitely a need for a renewed thrust for tackling this menace. In course of addressing the Naxal issue, both the central government and the affected state governments need unified and focused attention of every element of the government machinery to nullify the Naxal movement and at the same time bring inclusive development to the areas that are affected by the movement reflecting human rights, environment issues, livelihood, life and liberty of the tribal and marginalized sections of the society and development and security.

The contributors to this volume include people from 'ground zero' apart from those directly involved in the various state response mechanisms. It provides a constructive and pertinent insight into the consequences on the tribal population, the challenges for the Para-military forces as well as a perspective on the state's responses.

Lt. Gen. (Retd) V R Raghavan
President
Centre for Security Analysis

INTRODUCTION

Tejal Chandan and Ancy Joseph

The Carnegie Commission for Preventing Deadly Conflict emphasized "that economic growth, by itself, will not reduce prospects for violent conflict and could, in fact, be a contributing factor to internal conflicts".[1] Economic growth may generate prosperity but its inequitable and unbalanced nature can induce conflict through resentment and unrest. "The distribution of economic benefits in a society is a function of political decisions regarding the kind of economic system a society will construct... Poverty is often a structural outgrowth of these decisions, and when poverty runs in parallel with ethnic or cultural lines, it often creates a flashpoint".[2] In referring to the linkage between inequitable economic growth and internal conflict the Commission reiterated the problem of 'structural violence' that increasingly characterizes the nature of conflicts in several states.[3]

"Laws that are legitimately derived, widely promulgated and understood; a consistent, visible, fair, and active network of police authority to enforce the laws; an independent, equitable, and accessible grievance redress system, including above all an impartial judicial system and a penal system that is fair and prudent in meting out punishment"[4] form the basic elements of a strategy that seeks to deal with this problem. However

---

[1] David A. Hamburg and Cyrus R. Vance, Preventing Deadly Conflict, Final Report of the Carnegie Commission on Preventing Deadly Conflict, (New York: Carnegie Corporation, 1997), p-84.

[2] Ibid.

[3] Structural Violence refers to a form of violence based on the systemic ways in which a given social structure or social institution harms people by preventing them from meeting their basic needs.

[4] Hamburg and Vance, Preventing Deadly Conflict, p-81.

repeated, clichéd and 'hard to achieve' these may seem, they nevertheless form the crux of an internal security policy that requires constant attention through democratic processes.

The burgeoning 'Naxalite' conflict in India resonates some of the underlying notions about structural violence that results from inequitable growth and a faltering systemic and administrative policy. India's remarkable economic growth story with a post global economic slowdown GDP of 8 percent [5] represents extraordinary economic development opportunities along with one of the world's fastest widening social inequalities where the rich get richer and the poor get poorer. The marginalized population of the country fed into the growth of the Naxalite movement which began as a pro-poor and anti land lord movement in the 1960s and developed into its present form as a violent agitation that does not even spare the very people it once stood for. Although the agitation is only the latest manifestation of peasant struggles that have periodically emerged in India, it is sustained by the systematic neglect and ignorance of the grievances on the part of the government. The Naxalite movement has proliferated under these circumstances. Today the movement uses the grievances of the most affected population of the country i.e. the Tribals to wage a people's war against the state often colluding with certain elements of the state whenever necessary and advantageous and resists development as it threatens their entrenchment. As the intensity of the movement increased it gradually became the core internal security threat facing the country.

Although much has changed in terms of the ideology, organization and strategy of the groups that form a part of the movement, the same cannot be said of the government's attitude and fundamental response to the problem. While there have been prompt changes in policies to favor private investment, industrial growth, infrastructural development and agricultural exports, initiatives for land reform, rehabilitation and resettlement policies, poverty alleviation and protection against corruption and discrimination

---

[5] Ministry of Finance, " State of the Economy and Prospects", Economic Survey 2010-2011, (New Delhi: Government of India, 2011), p1, URL: http://indiabudget.nic.in/es2010-11/echap-01.pdf , Accessed on 1 March 2011.

have been much slower.[6] There is recognition of the grievances that have caused the problem but the response seems to rest heavily on the security aspects rather than the socio-economic aspects.

This book brings together five distinct papers presented at a seminar titled "The Naxal Threat: Causes, State Responses and Consequences" organized by the Centre for Security Analysis in August 2010. The following parts of this chapter discuss a few additional but alternative aspects on the subject and proceed towards introducing the key arguments of the authors in this volume.

Taxonomy

The term Naxalism is applied to a whole range of currents that trace their lineage back to the Naxalbari Revolt in 1967. Out of the various groups that adopted some form of Marxist- Leninist tag to describe themselves, two of them (Peoples' War group (PWG) and the Maoist Communist Centre (MCC)) merged to form the Communist Party of India (Maoist) in 2004.[7] This marked a watershed in the history of the Naxalite movement as it provided greater organizational cohesion and more concerted action for the objective of establishing the 'Red Corridor' from North Bihar to the underdeveloped hinterland of Jharkhand, Orissa, Chhattisgarh, Andhra Pradesh, Maharashtra and Karnataka. It is this merged entity that forms the subject of discussion and the object of the State's response. However, there is a practice of conflating all the currents that emerged from Naxalbari into one over arching term called Left-Wing Extremism. Aditya Nigam has argued that most of the Naxalite groups and parties have moved away from the "politics of nihilistic armed violence that distinguishes the CPI (Maoist)".[8] Tarring them all with the same brush, according to him, is not

---

[6] I. Basu, "Security and Development – Are they Two Sides of the Same Coin?: Investigating India's Two-Pronged Policy Towards Left Wing Extremism", Contemporary South Asia, 19 (4): 2011 (Forthcoming), URL: http://www.bath.ac.uk/cds/events/sym-papers/Basu2.pdf, Accessed on 21 February 2011.

[7] Aditya Nigam, "The Problem", Seminar, 607: March 2010, URL: http://www.india-seminar.com/2010/607/607_the_problem.htm, Accessed on 18 February 2011.

[8] Ibid.

only simplistic but also destructive as it will add to a bloated sense of the Maoist strength while marginalizing all other tendencies. This understanding is important as the response that the Government has been undertaking rests on distinguishing between the 'offender' who will face the coercive arm and the 'victim' who will face the welfare arm.

Change in the Cardinal Principle

The character of the Naxals has also transformed over the years. Today the Naxals are a modern guerilla force, logistically better organized, trained and more motivated to achieve their goal of liberating the country. The most worrisome aspect of the rising naxalite tide is the increasing militarization of the cadres of the CPI (Maoist).[9] The nexus of the naxalite groups with other extremist organizations has added to the complexity of the problem. The quantitative leap also led to a qualitative leap tangentially away from its predecessor the CPI (ML) which was founded by Charu Mazumdar. Mazumdar's key slogans were "integration with the masses" and "politics of command".[10] He emphasized the importance of relying on the masses for unleashing a militant peasant movement. The CPI (M), however, has no qualms about its dependence on big money and its obsession with war "has isolated the armed dimension (the element of squad activities) from the mass dimension (the element of broad peasant movement)".[11] The CPI (M) also has a stake in which party forms the government and hence participates indirectly and secretively in electoral politics often by supporting one ruling or would-be-ruling party against another, based on whoever is conceived as the 'main enemy' of the moment. Evidence of mutual support between Naxalites and political parties has emerged not only from Andhra Pradesh but also in the states of Bihar, Jharkhand and West Bengal. In effect this collusion between the state and the Naxalites damages the legitimacy of

---

[9] P V Ramana, "Spreading Naxalism - Napping Government", Indian Defence Review, 22 (1): 2007, URL:http://www.indiandefencereview.com/homeland%20security/Spreading-Naxalism—Napping-Government.html, Accessed on 3 February 2011.

[10] Arindam Sen. " Anarchism or Revolutionary Marxism", Seminar, 607: March 2010, URL:http://www.india-seminar.com/2010/607/607_arindam_sen.htm, Accessed on 18 February 2011

[11] Ibid.

the state and exposes the hypocrisy of the Naxals, their anti-state rhetoric and their actions. Another facet of the movement today is its individualistic work style and federative structure with the state and regional units operating autonomously, often leading to mistakes which are later admitted by top leaders.

The Securitization of Development

The state approaches the Naxalite movement as a "grave internal security threat' to its own legitimacy, stability and survival in vast swathes of the rural hinterland. Hence the policies that follow, aim at restoring the state's political legitimacy and weaning away the people from the Naxalites by winning them over with developmental initiatives. Thus in linking the need for development with that of the security of the state, the approach combines the law and order aspect with that of the socio-economic aspect. There are two potential implications of this linkage on the overall development agenda, there could be further coercive measures taken in the name of development or there could be a broadening of the security discourse, as is seen in the human security agenda.[12] In an attempt to restore its legitimacy, the government has relied on the coercive element of the response and has also sought to implement its development initiatives through the same approach. Through this prism, development achieves a sense of urgency that relies more on the visibility and pace of development activities often at the cost of pushing the continuing problems of poverty, inequality and displacement to the margins.[13] Hence the direction of development is skewed through the security-centric approach which effectively reduces the space for debate/ criticism of the existing economic and development policy that has caused the problem in the first place. The subject of change and reform affect the tribals and their way of life rather than the state's priorities of development and economic growth. In this context, it would be worth our while to recollect the concept of ' 'entrapment' – "a destructive process accompanying violent conflicts where the disputants come to believe that

---

[12] Basu, " Security and Development", p 3

[13] Ibid, p 5 and 28

far too much investment has gone into pursuing a particular line of action to quit or change policies that appear to have failed."[14] Do the government and the naxalite suffer from this phenomenon?

The Chapters

The chapters in this book trace the growth and causes of the Naxalite movement, analyze the government's responses, enlist and analyze the several laws and provisions provided by the government for the Tribals and examine the consequences of the conflict on the tribal way of life as well as the Central Reserve Police Force.

Sudha Ramachandran rightly relates the unmet needs and unattended grievances of the marginalized sections of India's vast population to the growth of the Naxalite movement. In the post liberalization period, several of the statutes of the Constitution have been violated and disregarded in the rush towards economic growth. The war waged between the security forces and Maoists has unleashed great human suffering accentuated by poverty which in turn trigger newer conflicts. Death and disappearance, illegal detention, extra judicial killings, forced displacement and a shattered livelihood is what the tribal faces on a daily basis. The complete breakdown of law and order has resulted in the militarization of the society due to the formation of private armies to combat Naxalites. She argues that the use of force by the State and the Maoists is deepening the intractability of the conflict. It has drawn more parties and vested interests into the conflict over the decades. The complexity of the conflict has grown with violence generating more problems. Her analysis of the state responses divulges the loopholes in the legislations promulgated by the Union government and the state governments. For instance in most of the states the law enforcement enabling rules are not in place, state governments are reluctant to operationalize the constitutional mandate or the respective gram sabhas are not empowered. She also examines the impact of Naxalism on the economy and investment climate in India. The minerals found in Naxalite affected regions contribute

---

[14] Pratul Ahuja and Rajat Ganguly, "The Fire Within: Naxalite Insurgency Violence in India " Small Wars and Insurgencies 18 no.2: 2007, p 272

to more than half the national mining production and are regarded crucial for India to continue to maintain its current levels of economic growth.

P V Ramana explores the responses of the Union and state governments to combat Naxalism. He argues that there is no clear and concrete road map to deal with the Naxals. The challenge of coordination is manifested not only in the multi-state nature of the problem but also the differences amongst the ruling parties on how to tackle the problem. He enlists various developmental programs of the government and points out the tardy implementation, weak monitoring and ineffective delivery of the goods. Political interference in fund allocation, among other issues is the key hurdle to effective implementation. He also points to the mismatch between the magnitude of the problem and the deployment of the forces, the need for a collective response that rises above a focus on the individual challenge of each state government and the need for a broad national political consensus among all the political parties within the affected states, among all states, and between the states and the Union Government.

E N Rammohan attributes the growth of the Naxalite movement to land alienation and caste discrimination. He traces the evolution of the Naxalite movement beginning in 1946 to its present form. He holds the opinion that the issue of Naxalism can only be settled to a large extent by bringing in and implementing land ceiling laws and giving opportunities to the poor and the tribals. While these laws should be implemented, the challenges that the state will face can be ascertained by reviewing the amount of land that is actually available for agricultural activities. This would in fact reveal that most of the lands that the government seeks to redistribute lie arid and would be of no use to farming and related activities.[15] Hence, justice along with an effective rehabilitation and resettlement program gains even further importance. *Rammohan* is of the view that the tribals are the final decision making authority on any developmental and mining activity in their homelands and recommends the use of security forces to enforce the

---

[15] Authors' conversation with Mr. Mohan Guruswamy, Centre for PolicyAlternatives, New Delhi at a discussion meeting on Internal Conflicts and Transnational Consequences-Phase II organized by the Centre for Security Analysis on 22-23 March, 2011

land ceiling laws and laws of the forest.

Although naxalite movement is spread over 20 states, the most acutely affected states happen to be Bihar, Chhatisgarh, Jharkhand, Orissa and West Bengal. These states feature dense forests with a predominance of tribal population followed by dalits and other backward communities. The tribals and dalits are among the poorest of the poor and the most socially marginalized sections of the society.[16] *Sharanya Nayak and Malini Subramaniam* look at Naxalism from perspectives of this most affected section of the Indian population. They assert that the loss of Tribal rights and livelihood began way back in Colonial India. This was further aggravated by the post independence governments of India. Some of these laws include *The Indian Forest Act of 1927, The Wildlife Protection Act of 1972*, which declared forests, degraded forests, waste lands on the periphery and even partly arable lands as reserved forests where human habitation was prohibited. *The Forest Conservation Act of 1980* and *The Biodiversity Act of 2002* restricted the use of forest land for non- forest purpose and herbal medicines for indigenous treatment respectively. With these, the local population that inhabited the forests and the adjoining lands actually became interlopers or encroachers on their own soil. There were revolts in the absence of reforms and ignorance of grievances and in such instances the attraction of a violent option grew tremendously.

Not all of the tribals chose to be a part of the movement. The irony is that in the present situation, the tribals bear the brunt of both the government's 'Operation Greenhunt' as well as the Naxalite's 'People's

---

[16] In fact, Bihar, Orissa, MP, Chhatisgarh, West Bengal, UP are states which account for 58% of the dalit population but 70% poor among them and 49% of tribal population but 63% of the poor among them.The percentage of dalits below poverty line was 36.8 (rural) and 40 (urban) and of tribals 47.3 (rural) and 33.3 (urban) compared to 28 (rural) and 25.77 (urban) for the nation. The incidence of poverty is higher than 50% among the tribals in Orissa (73%), Jharkhand (including Bihar 59%), MP (including Chhatisgarh 57%) and between 35-50% in West Bengal, Maharashtra, Assam and UP (including Uttaranchal). Similarly, the incidence of poverty is the highest in Bihar, Orissa, Madhya Pradesh, West Bengal, UP and Assam. The states of UP, MP (including Chhatisgarh), Bihar (including Jharkhand) and West Bengal have concentration of poor dalits. It is evident that neither the state intervention nor market liberalization policies have registered the desired impact on alleviation of poverty.

War'. They have to choose their sides in the absence of any other option. An alarming consequence of all of this is the criminalization and militarization of the tribal society. Furthermore, it is the tribals that form the lower rungs of the Naxalite cadres and are often the ones that meet the government's coercive arm. *Nayak and Subramaniam* bring out these aspects along with a discussion of the various pro-tribal laws that lack effective implementation.

The last chapter in this volume discusses the consequences on the force that is at the frontline of the government's response i.e. the Central Paramilitary Force (CPMF). *K S Sood* argues that the role of Paramilitary forces today has broadened with the inclusion, law and order, border management, election duty and disaster management along with of security and counter insurgency. While there has been a quantitative leap for the force in the form of a massive expansion, there has not been an equal qualitative leap. To add to this aspect is the acute shortage of officers, particularly in the rank of platoon and company commanders. He faults the constant outstretching of the force as one of the primary reasons for the mismatch between quantity and quality. *Sood* further points to the relentless political interference in the working of the Police and CPMF and discusses the crucial role of local police in the success of any counter-insurgency operation.

Going back to the Constitution

The need for a coercive approach arose with the rising levels of violence. However, these levels of violence should not undermine the importance of a well evaluated political and socio-economic approach. In the face of violence from all sides, the prospect of counter-violence holds great attraction for the grieved tribals and it is this attraction that sustains the movement.[17] In order to quell this attraction, analysts[18] urge the complete

---

[17] Aditya Nigam, " The Rumour of Maoism, Seminar, 607: March 2010, URL: http://www.india-seminar.com/2010/607/607_aditya_nigam.htm, accessed on 18 February 2011

[18] Analysts include autors from this book, Mr. E. N. Rammohan and Dr. P.V. Ramana as well as Mr. B. G. Verghese and Mr. M.R. Sivaraman who were a part of a Discussion Meeting on Internal Conflict and Transnational Consequences- Phase II, organized by the Centre for Security Analysis on 22-23 March 2011 to review the papers that were presented at the seminar on which this book is based.

implementation of Schedule V of the *Constitution of India*[19] in its letter and spirit. This part of the Constitution grants protection to the tribal people in Scheduled Areas in nine states in the country from alienation of their lands and natural resources to non-tribals.

Further, it is pertinent to note there is a great deal of uncertainty linked to the implementation of the various government schemes and programmes. Patience is the key to seeing a difference in the Naxalite affected states that will have to improve public service capacities and the delivery mechanisms for public goods. Manning the vacancies in the Indian Administrative Services in the affected states should get the right attention. Prime Minister Manmohan Singh pointed out at a Chief Minister's meet in July 2010, that without adequate and reasonably efficient staff, it would be difficult to implement any strategy or programme for the affected areas. [20]

---

[19] Schedule V is available in the annexure.

[20] Prime Minister's Office, " PM's Opening Remarks at the Meeting of Chief Ministers of Naxal Violence Affected States, 14 July, 2010, Government of India, URL:http://pmindia.nic.in/speech/content4print.asp?id=940, accessed on 18 February 2011

Annexure

FIFTH SCHEDULE

[Article 244(1)]

Provisions as to the Administration and Control of Scheduled Areas and Scheduled Tribes

PART A-GENERAL

1. Interpretation.-In this Schedule, unless the context otherwise requires, the expression "State" * * * .1does not include the [States of Assam. 2[Meghalaya, Tripura and Mizoram.3.]]]

2. Executive power of a State in Scheduled Areas.-Subject to the provisions of this Schedule, the executive power of a State extends to the Scheduled Areas therein.

3. Report by the Governor * * * .4 to the President regarding the administration of Scheduled Areas.-The Governor * * *.

4. of each State having Scheduled Areas therein shall annually, or whenever so required by the President, make a report to the President regarding the administration of the Scheduled Areas in that State and the executive power of the Union shall extend to the giving of directions to the State as to the administration of the said areas.

Provisions as to the Administration and Control of Scheduled Areas and Scheduled Tribes

PART B-ADMINISTRATION AND CONTROL OF SCHEDULED AREAS AND SCHEDULED TRIBES

4. Tribes Advisory Council.-(1) There shall be established in each State having Scheduled Areas therein and, if the President so directs, also in any State having Scheduled Tribes but not Scheduled Areas therein, a Tribes Advisory Council consisting of not more than twenty members of whom, as

nearly as may be, three-fourths shall be the representatives of the Scheduled Tribes in the Legislative Assembly of the State :

Provided that if the number of representatives of the Scheduled Tribes in the Legislative Assembly of the State is less than the number of seats in the Tribes Advisory Council to be filled by such representatives, the remaining seats shall be filled by other members of those tribes.

(2)It shall be the duty of the Tribes Advisory Council to advise on such matters pertaining to the welfare and advancement of the Scheduled Tribes in the State as may be referred to them by the Governor * * *.1. (3) The Governor * * * .

2 may make rules prescribing or regulating, as the case may be,—

(a) the number of members of the Council, the mode of their appointment and the appointment of the Chairman of the Council and of the officers and servants thereof,

(b) the conduct of its meetings and its procedure in general; and

(c) all other incidental matters.

5. Law applicable to Scheduled Areas.-(1) Notwithstanding anything in this Constitution the Governor 1* * * may by public notification direct that any particular Act of Parliament or of the Legislature of the State shall not apply to a Scheduled Area or any part thereof in the State or shall apply to a Scheduled Area or any part thereof in the State subject to such exceptions and modifications as he may specify in the notification and any direction given under this sub-paragraph may be given so as to have retrospective effect.

(2) The Governor may make regulations for the peace and good government of any area in a State which is for the time being a Scheduled Area. In particular and without prejudice to the generality of the foregoing power, such regulations may- (a)prohibit or restrict the transfer of land by or among members of the Scheduled Tribes in such area; (b)regulate the allotment of land to members of the Scheduled Tribes in such area; (c)regulate the carrying on of business as money-lender by persons who lend money to members of the Scheduled Tribes in such area.

(3)In making any such regulation as is referred to in subparagraph (2) of this paragraph, the Governor ***.3 may repeal or amend any Act of Parliament or of the Legislature of the State or any existing law which is for the time being applicable to the area in question.

(4)All regulations made under this paragraph shall be submitted forthwith to the President and, until assented to by him, shall have no effect.

(5)No regulation shall be made under this paragraph unless the Governor ***.4 making the regulation has, in the case where there is a Tribes Advisory Council for the State, consulted such Council.

PART C-SCHEDULED AREAS

6.Scheduled Areas.-(1) In this Constitution, the expression "Scheduled Areas" means such areas as the President may by order .1 declare to be Scheduled Areas.

(2) The President may at any time by order.2 - (a)direct that the whole or any specified part of a Scheduled Area shall cease to be a Scheduled Area or a part of such an area; [(aa).

3 increase the area of any Scheduled Area in a State after consultation with the Governor of that State;]

(b)alter, but only by way of rectification of boundaries, any Scheduled Area;

(c)on any alteration of the boundaries of a State or on the admission into the Union or the establishment of a new State, declare any territory not previously included in any State to be, or to form part of, a Scheduled Area;

[(d) rescind, in relation to any State or States, any order or orders made under this paragraph, and in consultation with the Governor of the State concerned, make fresh orders redefining the areas which are to be Scheduled Areas;] and any such order may contain such incidental and consequential provisions as appear to the President to be necessary and proper, but save as aforesaid, the order made under sub-paragraph (1) of this paragraph shall not be varied by any subsequent order.

PART D-AMENDMENT OF THE SCHEDULE

7. Amendment of the Schedule.-(I) Parliament may from time to time by law amend by way of addition, variation or repeal any of the provisions of this Schedule and, when the Schedule is so amended, any reference to this Schedule in this Constitution shall be construed as a reference to such Schedule as so amended.

(2)No such law as is Mentioned in sub-paragraph (1) of this paragraph shall be deemed to be an amendment of this Constitution for the purposes of article 368.

Fifth Schedule Areas

State	Areas
Andhra Pradesh	Visakhapatnam, East Godavari, West Godavari, Adilabad,Srikakulam, Vizianagaram, Mahboobnagar, Prakasam (only some mandals are scheduled mandals)
Jharkhand	Dumka, Godda, Devgarh, Sahabgunj, Pakur, Ranchi, Singhbhum (East&West), Gumla, Simdega, Lohardaga, Palamu, Garwa, (some districts are only partly tribal blocks)
Chattisgarh	Sarbhuja, Bastar, Raigad, Raipur, Rajnandgaon, Durg, Bilaspur, Sehdol, Chindwada, Kanker
Himachal Pradesh	Lahaul and Spiti districts, Kinnaur, Pangi tehsil and Bharmour sub-tehsil in Chamba district
Madhya Pradesh	Jhabua, Mandla, Dhar, Khargone, East Nimar (khandwa), Sailana tehsil in Ratlam district, Betul, Seoni, Balaghat, Morena
Gujarat	Surat, Bharauch, Dangs, Valsad, Panchmahl, Sadodara, Sabarkanta (partsof these districts only)
Maharashtra	Thane, Nasik, Dhule, Ahmednagar, Pune, Nanded, Amravati, Yavatmal, Gadchiroli, Chandrapur (parts of these districts only)
Orissa	Mayurbhanj, Sundargarh, Koraput (fully scheduled area in these threedistricts), Raigada, Keonjhar, Sambalpur, Boudhkondmals, Ganjam, Kalahandi, Bolangir, Balasor (parts of these districts only)
Rajasthan	Banswara, Dungarpur (fully tribal districts), Udaipur, Chittaurgarh, Siroi (partly tribal areas)

THE MAOIST CONFLICT IN DANDAKARANYA

Sudha Ramachandran

Discourse on India's Maoist conflict is suffused with black and white images and interpretations. Since 2004, India's Prime Minister Manmohan Singh has repeatedly described the Maoist insurgency as the "gravest internal security challenge" facing the country.[1] The conflict is variously looked upon as a law and order problem by some, as a "fight for social justice, equality, protection, security and local development" by others.[2] While some perceive the State as protector and the Maoists as terrorists, others view the State as oppressor and the Maoists as savior. However, the picture on the ground reveals shades of grey. The Communist Party of India (Maoist) (CPI-Maoist), the main Maoist organization active today and the focus of this study, was declared a terrorist organization by the Government of India in June 2009.[3] Indeed, it does use violence against civilians that is aimed at terrorizing the larger population. However, comparable tactics have been used by other parties to the conflict as well. Vigilante groups like the Salwa Judum in Chhattisgarh that were set up or supported by the government have carried out similar attacks. The impact of the armed conflict has been

---

[1] "Naxalism Biggest Threat to Internal Security: Manmohan", The Hindu, May 24, 2010, http://www.thehindu.com/news/national/article436781.ece, accessed on September 10, 2010.

[2] Interestingly, this is a description of the Maoists in a report commissioned by the Planning Commission of the Indian government. See, Government of India, Planning Commission, Development Challenges in Extremist Affected Areas, Report of an Expert Group to Planning Commission, 2008, 59-60, available online at http://planningcommission.gov.in/reports/publications/rep_dce.pdf, accessed on July 12, 2010.

[3] Government of India, Press Information Bureau, "CPI (Maoist) included in list of terrorist organizations to avoid any ambiguity," June 22, 2009, available online at http://pib.nic.in/release/release.asp?relid=49325&kwd, accessed on September 10, 2010.

mixed too. While violence, which has reached unprecedented levels in recent years, has caused immense suffering, it has drawn attention to the situation of India's tribals and other marginalized groups, forcing the government to deal with the conflict's underlying causes.

The Maoists are active to varying degrees across the country.[4] This study focuses on the armed conflict in the Dandakaranya region. A thickly forested and hilly area, Dandakaranya includes the districts of Bastar, Dantewada and Kanker in Chhattisgarh; Gadchiroli and Chandrapur in Maharashtra; Koraput and Malkangiri in Orissa; and Adilabad, Karimnagar, Khammam and East Godavari districts in Andhra Pradesh (see map). The Dandakaranya region is mineral-rich. However, its people – predominantly from tribal communities - live in conditions of abject poverty. Referred to by the Maoists as the Dandakaranya Special Zone, this area is currently the focus of Operation Green Hunt, launched by the government to eliminate the Maoists.

This study seeks to capture some of the complexities of the Maoist conflict, especially its impact. It begins with a brief overview of the nature of the Maoist conflict and goes on to trace its evolution over the past several decades. This is followed by an examination of the roots of the conflict and the way the conflict is being waged by some of the main actors. Finally, the study explores the conflict's impact on people, policies and institutions. It draws attention to the human toll and the devastation it has wrought on lives and livelihoods of millions of people. It also looks at how the conflict has shaped the government's response, forcing it to prioritize socio-economic development of backward districts and look into issues like tribal land alienation and the mining policy. The study argues that the waging of violent conflict by the main adversaries – the State and the Maoists – is deepening the conflict and making it intractable and protracted.

---

[4] The Maoists are active mainly in a swathe of territory often referred to as the 'Red Corridor', which stretches from Karnataka in the south to include Andhra Pradesh, Maharashtra, Chhattisgarh, Jharkhand, West Bengal and Bihar. Other states affected by Maoist activity but to a lesser degree are Kerala, Madhya Pradesh, Uttar Pradesh and Uttarakhand.

Map of India showing the Dandakaranya region

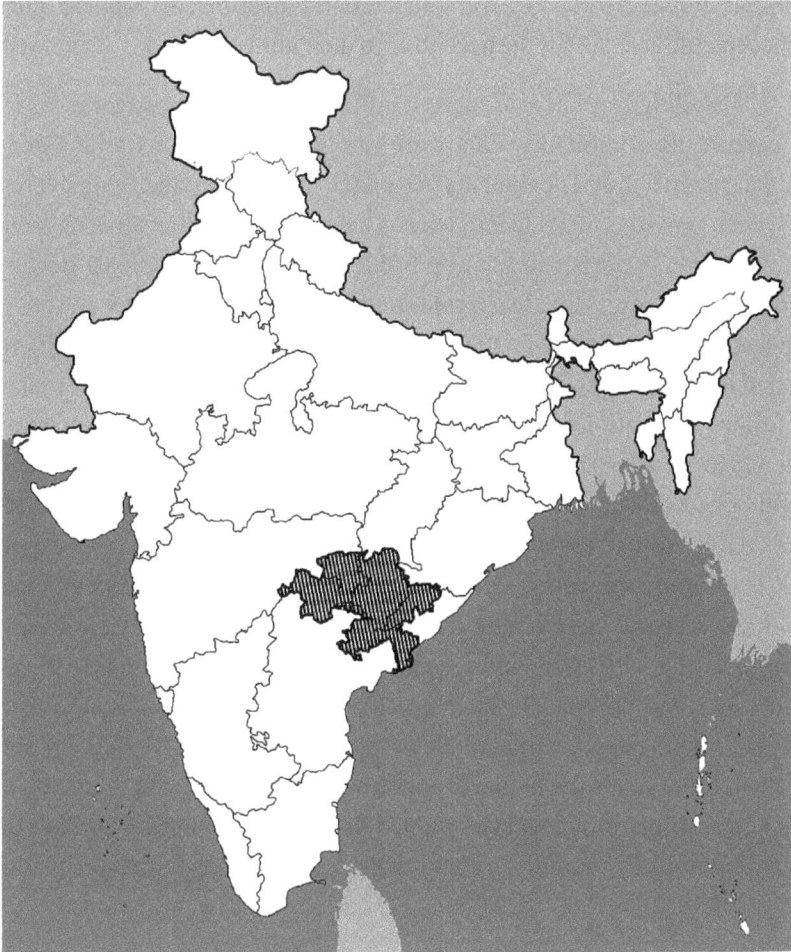

Understanding the Maoist Conflict

India's Maoist conflict is often described as one between the Maoists and the State, wherein the Maoists are seeking to capture State power. According to the Constitution of the CPI (Maoist), "The ultimate aim or maximum program of the party is the establishment of a communist society. This New Democratic Revolution will be carried out and completed through armed agrarian revolutionary war i.e. the Protracted People's War with area-wise seizure of power remaining as its central task."[5] This goal is seen to be incompatible with India's parliamentary democracy. Several ministerial statements and government reports stress that the Maoists' goal is unacceptable and call for the need to curb their armed struggle "at any cost."[6]

Analyzing conflict in terms of conflicting goals of the adversaries fails to capture its complexity. Goals are maximalist positions articulated in public statements and documents. An understanding of underlying interests, however, provides insights into what is keeping the conflict alive or driving the violence. A deeper delving into the Maoist conflict reveals powerful economic interests, not always admitted to by the various actors. Activists have accused the State of acting on behalf of mining companies and other vested interests. They allege that the motive behind the government's launch of military operations in mineral-rich tribal areas is to drive the inhabitants out. Once the area's tribal population is driven out, their argument goes, the Fifth Schedule of the Constitution, which designates the area as tribal land and thus rules out its sale to non-tribals, would no longer apply, freeing it for sale to mining companies.[7] Others have drawn links between corruption and conflict. With the government allocating vast sums of money for counter-insurgency operations and infrastructure-building in conflict zones, officials, politicians and contractors have a vested interest in keeping the conflict alive or magnifying the magnitude of the Maoist threat. After all, for many of them more funds mean more money available to divert to their personal pockets.[8] Similarly, it has been argued that economic interests rather than lofty revolutionary ambitions could be driving the Maoists' pursuit of armed

---

[5] Central Committee (P), CPI (Maoist), "Party Constitution,"available online at http://www.satp. org/satporgtp/countries/india/maoist/documents/papers/partyconstitution.htm, accessed on July 26, 2010.

[6] Government of India, Ministry of Home Affairs, Annual Report, 2009-10, 17, available online at http://www.mha.nic.in/pdfs/AR%28E%290910.pdf, accessed on September 19, 2010.

[7] Shoma Chaudhary, "Weapons of Mass Desperation," Tehelka, 6 no.39, October 3, 2009, available online at http://www.tehelka.com/story_main42.asp?filename=Ne031009 coverstory.asp, accessed on July 2, 2010.

[8] Rahul K. Bhonsle, "Naxalism: Everybody Loves a Good Insurgency," June 26, 2010, available online at http://cms.boloji.com/index.cfm?md=Blogs&sd=Blog&BlogID=151, accessed on September 14, 2010.

struggle as well. They are said to be extorting huge amounts as 'protection fee' from mining companies and contractors in areas under their control. This 'revenue' is believed to be an important factor behind the leadership's reluctance to give up arms and negotiate an end to the conflict.[9]

The Maoist conflict is often described as one pitting the rebels against the State, a conflict with only two actors. While the Maoists and the State are the two main adversaries, there are several other actors who are influencing the conflict's evolution and have a stake in its outcome. Tribals play a central role in the conflict in Dandakaranya. It is the structural violence that they experience that is driving the conflict. It is among them that much of the armed confrontation is unfolding. It is on their behalf that the Maoists claim to be waging war against the State and it is they who are bearing the brunt of the violence. Maoist cadres are overwhelmingly tribal but not all tribals are Maoists. Many prefer mass politics. While some tribals would like to keep their distance from the Maoists, others see them as a useful ally. There are tribals too who are anti-Maoist and work with the State.

There are other parties, too, such as mining companies, landlords, liquor mafias, etc., who have a vested interest in the conflict. Mining companies are anxious to extract minerals and are worried that the growing clout of the Maoists will hamper their business ambitions. They are said to be funding anti-Maoist militias. Some of these like the State-sponsored Salwa Judum in Chhattisgarh have unleashed horrific levels of violence, escalating the conflict and militarizing tribal society in Dantewada to unprecedented levels.

There are civil society activists and organizations too, whose work is affecting and being affected by the conflict. While some are neutral, others are providing support to one side or the other. There are public intellectuals and activists who are drawing attention to human rights violations by the adversaries. Their interventions have served to put pressure on the Maoists, militias and the State to refrain from targeting civilians. There is

---

[9] Nishit Dholabhai, "Govt. Puts Credible Talks Onus on Maoists", The Telegraph,August 26, 2010, available online at http://www.telegraphindia.com/1100826/jsp/nation/story_12857602.jsp, accessed on September 14, 2010.

the corporate media too, which has endorsed the government's position and strategy, prejudicing the public against the Maoists.[10]

None of the parties to the conflict is a homogenous entity. Sharp differences on strategy are evident at the highest levels of government and between the central and various state governments.[11] There are tensions and contradictions too between the largely urban, educated middle-class Maoist leadership and the rank and file, which is tribal or low caste/Dalit, on strategy and tactics as well as objectives. Lower-level commanders and fighters are said to be keen on land reforms and livelihood security rather than the overthrow of the State.

The Maoist conflict is an armed conflict, although the government has denied that it is one under international law.[12] According to the Uppsala Conflict Data Program, "armed conflict is a contested incompatibility that concerns government and/or territory where the use of armed force between two parties, of which at least one is the government of a state, results in

---

[10] Sevanti Ninan, "Media Matters: Assembly-line news," The Hindu, October 11, 2009, available online at http://www.thehindu.com/opinion/columns/Sevanti_Ninan/article32256.ece, accessed on September 14, 2010.

[11] There has been considerable opposition, for instance, to Home Minister P Chidambaram's focus on the military approach to dealing with Maoists from others within the ruling Congress party, especially from Congress General Secretary Digvijay Singh. See Singh's article, "Rethink Counter-Maoist Strategy: Digvijay Singh to P Chidambaram," Economic Times, April 14, 2010, available online at http://economictimes.indiatimes.com/news/politics/nation/Rethink-counter-Maoist-strategy-Digvijay-Singh-to-P-Chidambaram/articleshow/5800173.cms, accessed on September 18, 2010.

[12] "Naxal Problem Not an Armed Conflict, India tells UN", Times of India, June18, 2010, available online at http://timesofindia.indiatimes.com/india/Naxal-problem-not-an-armed-conflict-India-tells-UN/articleshow/6063604.cms, accessed on June 20, 2010. Often governments deny being engaged in an armed conflict even when they obviously are because an internal armed conflict signals failure and inadequacy on their part. More importantly, "once that [armed conflict] threshold is crossed, international humanitarian law applies and domestic law is circumscribed. In international armed conflicts, the regular armed forces of a state become legitimate targets. In all armed conflict, the International Committee of the Red Cross (ICRC) may demand the right to visit detainees and to demand that certain standards applicable to detention are maintained." Mary Ellen O'Connell, "Defining Armed Conflict,"Journal of Conflict & Security Law, 13 (December 10, 2008), available online at http://ssrn.com/abstract=1392211, accessed on July 10, 2010.

at least 25 battle-related deaths in one calendar year."[13] By this definition, the Maoist conflict qualifies to be called an armed conflict, the fatalities having crossed the annual armed conflict benchmark of 25 every year over the past four decades. According to official data, the number of fatalities in 2009 was 908. Data collated by the South Asia Terrorism Portal puts the figure at 998 fatalities, just short of the high-intensity conflict benchmark of 1,000 fatalities per year. Thus, the conflict is not just an armed conflict but one that is on the brink of becoming a high intensity conflict.[14] In fact, some analysts describe the conflict as a civil war.[15]

Evolution of the Conflict

Conflicts pass through various phases. Broadly, these include the latent phase, conflict emergence, escalation, hurting stalemate, de-escalation, settlement/resolution, post-conflict peace-building and reconciliation. However, rarely do conflicts move in a linear fashion from one phase to another. Phases are skipped; an escalating conflict could de-escalate without passing through a stalemate. While de-escalation must precede conflict resolution, it need not necessarily lead to the latter. Reversions to an earlier phase are not uncommon. A period of de-escalation, when negotiations or even a resolution seem in sight, may be followed by a sudden escalation in the conflict.

The Maoist conflict has persisted for several decades. It has escalated and de-escalated, waxed and waned over time. The present escalation phase, the focus of this study, is the most intense so far.

The origins of the Indian Maoist movement can be traced back to the 1946-51 period, when Indian Communists, inspired by Chairman Mao's 'people's war', took up armed struggle in rural Telangana to free peasants from feudal rule. Led by the Communist Party of India (CPI), the agrarian

---

[13] Uppsala University, "Conflict Definitions,"available online at http://www.pcr.uu.se/research/UCDP/data_and_publications/definitions_all.htm, accessed on July 15, 2010

[14] South Asia Terrorism Portal (SATP), " South Asia Assessment 2010,"available online at http://www.satp.org/satporgtp/southasia/index.html, accessed on July 20, 2010.

[15] Amalendu Misra, "Subaltern and the Civil War: An Assessment of Left-wing Insurgency in South Asia," Civil Wars, 5, no. 4 (Winter 2002): 56-58.

uprising was initially organized around simple demands against eviction of peasants from their land. When met with the combined repression by landlords and the Nizam's administrative machinery, it quickly expanded into a movement for overthrow of Nizam's rule.[16] With India sending its troops into Hyderabad, Nizam's rule ended and the princely state came under Indian rule. The movement then went underground and the Communists found refuge in the thick forests of northern Andhra. It was during this period that the revolutionaries began working with the tribals, laying the foundation for the subsequent focus of the Maoists on tribal deprivation.[17] Meanwhile, the government of Prime Minister Jawaharlal Nehru abolished the zamindari system and promised to undertake a series of land reforms, leading to the CPI joining mainstream parliamentary politics in 1951.[18] The armed conflict de-escalated thereafter, although the issues underlying it remained unresolved.

In 1967, the conflict erupted in an armed uprising in Naxalbari in West Bengal,[19] when the henchmen of local landlords assaulted a tribal sharecropper. The tribals retaliated by attacking the landlords and claiming their land. The uprising in Naxalbari was crushed quickly by the State through use of force but it spread to other parts of West Bengal, Bihar and Andhra Pradesh. In 1969, the Communist Party of India (Marxist-Leninist) [CPI(ML)] was set up, giving the insurgency a command structure. It made rapid gains initially but began weakening on account of tactical errors by its leaders. Brutal police and paramilitary operations too contributed to undermining it[20] and by 1975, it had all but collapsed. Most of its leaders

---

[16] Mohan Ram, "The Telengana Peasant Armed Struggle, 1946-51," Economic and Political Weekly (EPW), 8, no. 23 (June 9, 1973): 1025-32.

[17] For a ringside view of the revolutionaries' work in this period, see P. Sundarayya, Telangana People's Struggle and its Lessons (New Delhi: Foundation Books, 2006).

[18] For a detailed account of the circumstances that led to the withdrawal of the armed struggle, see note 16 above.

[19] It is from the name 'Naxalbari' that the terms 'Naxalites' or 'Naxals' - as Indian Maoists are often called - are drawn. This essay will use the terms 'Naxalite' and 'Maoist' interchangeably as it will 'tribal', 'Adivasi' and 'Scheduled Tribe'.

[20] Sumanta Banerjee, India's Simmering Revolution: The Naxalite Uprising (London: Zed Books, 1984) and Biplab Dasgupta, The Naxalite Movement (Bombay: Allied Publishers, 1974). For an account of the impact of Naxalites'armed campaign in rural India, see Biplab Dasgupta, "Naxalite Armed Struggles and the Annihilation Campaign in Rural Areas," EPW, 8, no. 4/6 (Feb 1973): 173-75, 179, 181, 183, 185-88.

were killed or in jail and thousands of sympathizers – many of them students and intellectuals - were in custody. The remnants were scattered around the country. The setbacks prompted the surviving leaders to review their strategy. While some advocated mass politics and participation in parliamentary elections, others gave primacy to armed struggle.[21]

The Maoist conflict escalated again a few years later. In 1980, Kondapalli Seetharamaiah formed the People's War Group (PWG) in Andhra Pradesh. The Maoist Communist Centre (MCC) emerged in Bihar a few years later. These two groups dominated the armed struggle in the decades that followed. In the early years of its existence, the PWG built mass organizations among youth, peasants and women but soon it moved exclusively to armed struggle and expanded its area of operation beyond Andhra to include parts of northern Karnataka, eastern Maharashtra, southern Chhattisgarh and Orissa.[22] It started the Dandakaranya Adivasi Kisan Mazdoor Sangathan (DAKMS) and the Krantikari Adivasi Mahila Sanghatan (KAMS) in Dantewada in the early 1980s. DAKMS raised issues like access to land and forests, fair wages for *tendu* leaf (used in rolling *beedis* or handmade cigarettes smoked widely in South Asia) pickers and better prices for non-timber forest produce – issues that struck a chord with the tribals. This helped the PWG build a support base across Dandakaranya. *Sanghams* were set up to replace the traditional structures of authority at the village level and *gram rajya* committees to settle village disputes and delegate developmental work. Guerrilla squads or *dalams* too emerged.[23] Even as the PWG's influence and presence in the Dandakaranya forest was being consolidated, the movement was weakened by fratricidal warfare.

---

[21] Sumanta Banerjee, "Beyond Naxalbari,"Economic and Political Weekly (July 22-28, 2006): 3159-63.

[22] Venkitesh Ramakrishnan, "The Road from Naxalbari,"Frontline, 22, no, 21, Oct 8-21, 2005, available online at http://www.flonnet.com/fl2221/stories/20051021008801000.ht, accessed on July 21, 2010.

[23] Nandini Sundar, "Bastar, Maoism and Salwa Judum," Economic and Political Weekly, 41, no. 29 (July 22, 2006): 3189, available online at http://www.cjpkar.org/wp-content/uploads/2009/12/Bastar-Maoism-and-Salwa-Judum.pdf, accessed on July 21, 2010.

The latest phase of escalation in the Maoist conflict began in the late 1990s. It received a substantial boost in 2004 with the merger of the PWG and the MCC to form the Communist Party of India (Maoist). The PWG had been working on bringing various Maoist groups under its umbrella right from the early 1980s but it was only in the late 1990s that these efforts began paying off. In 1998, CPI-ML (Party Unity) merged with the PWG, strengthening the latter's presence in Bihar and thus providing it with links to the Nepali Maoists. In 2001, nine South Asian Maoist groups including the PWG, the MCC and the Communist Party of Nepal (Maoists) formed the Coordinating Committee of Maoist Parties of South Asia (CCOMPOSA), giving a fillip to the creation of a "Compact Revolutionary Zone" extending from Andhra to Nepal, and enabling logistical co-operation and tactical co-ordination among them.

The merger of the PWG and the MCC gave the hitherto deeply divided Indian Maoist movement a semblance of unity. As a result of the merger, there is a unified command structure in place today and although the Maoists are spread out over several states, they have an all-India character and perspective. There is far more co-ordination and co-operation between Maoists in different parts of the country than ever before. If in the past, much of their energy was consumed by fratricidal fighting and turf wars, the merger has enabled them to focus their firepower on the State. The coming together of the PWG and the MCC, which until their merger accounted for 88 percent of the countrywide Maoist violence and 89 percent of the resultant deaths, created "a formidable threat and challenge [to the government]". [24] It gave a boost to Maoist logistics, facilitating movement of fighters, weapons and funds along a stretch of territory running from Karnataka to Bihar and beyond to Nepal.

The merger has contributed to a sharp increase in Maoist capacity in recent years. Their numbers have increased manifold as has the sophistication of their weaponry. Attacks have grown in frequency and magnitude.

---

[24] Government of India, Ministry of Home Affairs Annual Report, 2008-09, 16, available online at http://www.mha.nic.in/pdfs/AR%28E%290809.pdf , accessed on July 25, 2010.

Table 1

Number of Maoist-related Incidents, 2002-2009

Year	2002	2003	2004	2005	2006	2007	2008	2009
Number of Incidents	1465	1597	1533	1608	1509	1565	1591	2258

Source: Government of India, Ministry of Home Affairs, *Annual Report, 2005-06; Annual Report, 2008-09; Annual Report, 2009-10.*

In previous escalatory phases, Maoist operations were largely hit-and-run attacks, targeting 'class enemies' i.e. landlords, moneylenders and police informers. In the present phase, their attacks are far more sophisticated and deadly. They have targeted several high-profile personalities. Andhra Pradesh Chief Minister Chandrababu Naidu, among the most tightly guarded politicians in the country, escaped a landmine attack near Tirupati in 2003. They have executed several meticulously planned jailbreaks, including the one at Jehanabad in Bihar in 2005 when they freed 350 of their jailed comrades. They have raided armories and camps of the police and paramilitary forces. The Maoists have repeatedly signaled their capacity to stand and fight the security forces. In 2009, they stormed the government-owned National Aluminum Company Ltd. (NALCO) in Koraput and battled paramilitary forces for nine hours before retreating. In April 2010, in what is among the deadliest of Maoist attacks in terms of fatalities, 76 personnel of the Central Reserve Police Force (CRPF) were killed in an ambush at Chintalnar in Dantewada. The Maoists are believed to have massed around 600 cadres at the site of the attack. That they were able to mass such a large number of fighters in an area where the security forces were present, without arousing the suspicions of the latter signals their formidable capacity for planning and executing major operations today.

The scale of the State's anti-Maoist operations too has grown enormously during the present period of escalation. In previous escalatory phases, it was the state police that was at the forefront of anti-Maoist operations. There was little inter-state co-ordination, allowing Maoists to flee across state borders when pursued. That has changed with the central government launching Operation Green Hunt simultaneously in several states. Paramilitary forces have been deployed. The magnitude of this operation is unprecedented. In Bastar zone alone, a 40,000 square kilometer area, 14 battalions of the CRPF – each made up of around 1,000 men – besides five battalions of the Border Security Force have been inducted. In addition, there are some 5,000 police and seven battalions of armed police in Bastar.[25] Calls for deployment of the Indian Army in the Maoist areas are growing. This demand has been turned down by the government for now, although army officers will be involved in strategizing operations. Helicopters of the Indian Air Force are providing logistical support but the possibility of their use in combat against Maoists in the near future cannot be ruled out. Already they have been granted permission "to fire in self-defense." This has the potential of seriously escalating the conflict.[26]

In the earlier phases of conflict escalation too, Maoists did target civilians. Landlords and money lenders who were seen to be exploiting the poor were killed. Villagers thought to be police informers were labeled 'traitors' and executed. However, the Maoists refrained from carrying out attacks that would result in high civilian casualties. That has now changed with the frequency and magnitude of attacks on 'soft targets' escalating in recent years. In May 2010, a private passenger bus was blown up by Maoists at Chingawaram in Dantewada, killing 31 people, mainly civilians. The Maoists, subsequently, sought to justify this attack by claiming that

---

[25] Praveen Swami, "The Seduction of Maximum Force," The Hindu, May 31, 2010, available online at http://beta.thehindu.com/opinion/lead/article442994.ece?homepage=true, accessed on July 15, 2010 and Saikat Dutta, "On War Footing, Outlook, Oct 26, 2009, available online at http://www.outlookindia.com/article.aspx?262350, accessed on July 15, 2010.

[26] IAF choppers have come under fire twice so far; in Pedia in Bastar in November 2008 and then in Gadchiroli a few months later. For implications of the permission to IAF " to fire in self-defense,"see Sudha Ramachandran, "Chopper ruling raises Maoist tensions, Asia Times Online, August 17, 2010, available online at http://www.atimes.com/atimes/South_Asia/LH17Df04.html, accessed on September 18, 2010.

11 Special Police Officers (SPOs) were travelling in the bus and that the government was using civilians as human shields. A senior Maoist leader in the south Dandakaranya region said civilian deaths "could not be helped", signaling that the Maoists now see civilian casualties as inevitable and acceptable collateral damage in their war against the State.[27]

As for the State, in previous phases of escalation it did arrest or kill civilians thought to be Maoist sympathizers. Many villagers and students were killed in the course of anti-Maoist operations and many civilians in Maoist areas were drawn into the battle as police informers. However, in recent years, the State has been arming civilians as part of a planned strategy to fight the Maoists.[28] This has taken the armed conflict to a new, higher level. In June 2005, a supposedly spontaneous uprising against Maoists called Salwa Judum emerged in Bastar and Dantewada. Subsequent events revealed that there was little spontaneous about Salwa Judum; it was a government-sponsored strategy that involved arming tribal youth, including children, and surrendered Maoists to fight the Maoists. Government forces and Salwa Judum activists jointly raided villages. They unleashed violence on an unprecedented scale, torturing, raping and killing villagers, looting their homes and burning down entire villages.[29]

---

[27] 'Azad' quoted in The Telegraph, May 19, 2010 available online at http://www.telegraphindia. com/1100519/jsp/nation/story_12464820.jsp, accessed on July 12, 2010.

[28] In 1990, an anti Naxal group called Jan Jagran Abhiyan (JJA) was set up in Chhattisgarh by MLA Mahendra Karma. The JJA threatened villagers to hand over sangham members or else face punishment. Punishment involved beating, rape and killing of villagers, looting and burning of their homes. The JJA had the moral support of the Bharatiya Janata Party (BJP) and the CPI. See People's Union of Civil Liberties (PUCL), When the state makes war on its own people: A report on the violation of people's rights during the Salwa Judum campaign in Dantewada, Chhattisgarh, (New Delhi: PUCL, 2006), 11-12, available online at http://www. pucl.org/Topics/Human-rights/2006/salwa_judum.pdf, accessed on July 29, 2010. "The JJA was morally supported by BJP leadership, but there was no official funding or arms given from the state." Jason Miklian, "The Purification Hunt: The Salwa Judum Counterinsurgency in Chhattisgarh, India,"Dialectical Anthropology, 33, nos. 3-4 (December 2009): 447.

[29] Ramachandra Guha, Harivansh, Farah Naqvi, E. A. S. Sarma, Nandini Sundar and B. G. Verghese, "War in the Heart of India: Excerpts from the Report by the Independent Citizens' Initiative,"Social Scientist, 34, no. 7/8 (July-August 2006): 47-61; PUCL, "When the state makes war"and Miklian, "The Purification Hunt,"441-59

As the above discussion indicates, the Maoist conflict has persisted for several decades, de-escalating from time to time, only to re-emerge and escalate subsequently. Every escalation seems to be of a greater magnitude than the one before. The protracted nature of the conflict and its intensity in the present phase indicates that this is not a mere 'law and order' problem. The conflict has its roots in socio-economic and political grievances, which have not been addressed.[30] This explains its repeated escalation and intractability.

Roots of the Conflict

Human needs theorists have drawn attention to the central role that unmet human needs play in triggering conflict. According to them, conflict is generated when people feel their basic needs for security, identity, well-being, self-determination and so on are being denied or under threat. When social, political and economic structures, institutions and policies prevent people from meeting these needs, they are being subjected to structural violence, writes peace psychologist Daniel Christie.[31] Structural violence provokes resistance, "violent resistance if necessary," points out human needs theorist John Burton.[32] Drawing attention to the link between unmet human needs, structural violence and violent conflict, he observes that "individuals are prepared to go to extreme lengths to defy systems in order to pursue their deeply felt needs, even death by suicide bombing or hunger strikes."[33]

---

[30] Following the Naxalbari uprising, India's Home Ministry compiled a report called The Causes and Nature of Current Agrarian Tensions, which acknowledged: "The basic cause of unrest, namely, the defective implementation of laws enacted to protect the interests of the tribals, remains; unless this is attended to, it would not be possible to win the confidence of the tribals whose leadership has been taken over by the extremists." Sumanta Banerjee points out that if several decades after that report was compiled officials are still repeating the same issues at meetings, i.e. that the conflict is not a law and order issue but a socio-economic problem, "it is because the Indian state has progressed little, and learnt still less from past experiences." Sumanta Banerjee, "Naxalbari: Between Past and Future," EPW, 37, no. 22 (June 1-7, 2002): 2115-16.

[31] Daniel J. Christie, "Reducing Direct and Structural Violence: The Human Needs Theory," Peace and Conflict: The Journal of Peace Psychology, 3 no 4 (1997): 323.

[32] John W. Burton, Violence Explained (New York: St Martin's Press, 1997), 33.

[33] Ibid., 19.

Structural violence lies at the heart of India's Maoist conflict. Structural violence is said to have occurred when people have been systematically deprived of material and non-material resources necessary for humans to reach their potential. In Dandakaranya, institutions and policies are not just standing in the way of tribals tapping their potential but worse, their most basic needs such as those for food, security and survival are not being met. So severe is the structural violence that has been unleashed on the tribals in this region that people here are dying of poverty, starvation and treatable illnesses.

It is to the tribals' loss of land and thus of their homes, livelihood and means of survival that the grievances fuelling the conflict can be traced. The Nehruvian development paradigm envisaged rapid industrialization of the country. The building of big dams and setting up of heavy industries was given priority, a policy best encapsulated by Nehru's description of dams as "the temples of modern India".[34] Millions of tribals were displaced by big dams, hydroelectric projects and public sector mining activity in this period. Besides, legislation restricted their access to forests and common property resources.[35] This displacement has accelerated under economic liberalization, with tribals being displaced to enable mineral extraction, and the setting up of industries and Special Economic Zones (SEZs).

India's adoption of neo-liberal economic policies from the early 1990s onwards has accelerated the country's economic growth rate, increased the number of millionaires and expanded the size of the middle class in the country. However, it has worsened the condition of the rural poor. With the government cutting back on investment in the social sector, the deprivation suffered by the rural poor has intensified over the past two decades. Particularly devastating has been the impact of neo-liberal policies on tribals living in mineral-rich areas. An examination of India's mining policy and its impact on tribals is essential to understand why the condition

---

[34] Ramachandra Guha, India after Gandhi: The History of the Worlds Largest Democracy (New Delhi: Pan Macmillan, Picador, 2008), 212-13.

[35] Kannan Kasturi, "Whose land is 'wasteland'?," InfoChange News & Features, April 2008, available online at http://infochangeindia.org/200804037059/Agenda/Battles-Over-Land/Whose-land-is-%E2%80%98wasteland%E2%80%99.html, accessed on July 14, 2010.

of tribals in mineral-rich Dandakaranya is so wretched.

Prior to liberalization, extraction and refining of minerals was largely undertaken by the government. This changed with the National Mineral Policy of March 1993, which opened the doors to foreign direct investment (FDI) in the mining sector. The process for FDI was eased in 1997 and since 2006, 100 percent FDI is being permitted in mining. Liberalization of investment in the mining sector has opened the floodgates to mining companies especially in mineral-rich Chhattisgarh, Orissa and Jharkhand. With investment pouring in, permits are being issued for mineral extraction on tribal land in violation of legislations and court judgments that forbid sale of tribal land to non-tribals.[36]

Since the opening up of the mining sector to FDI, thousands of acres of forest land have been diverted for non-forest use. Such diversion shot up from 789 hectares at the end of 1993-94 to 28,769 hectares a decade later, an average annual increase of 43 percent. A third of this diversion was for mining activity.[37] Much of the mineral-rich land in Chhattisgarh, Orissa and Jharkhand is tribal land, land guaranteed to them under the Constitution's Fifth Schedule. Yet, in violation of the Fifth Schedule and of a historic Supreme Court judgment in 1997, often referred to as the Samata judgment,[38] several thousands of acres of tribal land is being handed over to

[36] Prafulla Das, "Mines of conflict," Frontline, 22, no. 24, November 19-December 02, 2005, available online at http://www.flonnet.com/fl2224/stories/20051202002304000.htm, last accessed on July 15, 2010; Aman Sethi, "Dark side of mining," Frontline, 24 , no. 9 , May 5-18, 2007, available online at http://www.frontline.in/fl2409/stories/20070518001604200.htm, accessed on July 15, 2010; Venkitesh Ramakrishnan, "Plunder & profit," Frontline, 27, no. 14 , July 3-16, 2010, available online at http://www.flonnet.com/fl2714/stories/20100716271400400.htm, accessed on July 15, 2010 and Ajoy Ashirwad Mahaprashasta, "FDI vs Tribes,"Frontline,27, no. 14, July 3-16, 2010, available online at http://www.flonnet.com/fl2714/stories/20100716271401405.htm, accessed on July 20, 2010.

[37] Banikanta Mishra, "Agriculture, Industry and Mining in Orissa in the Post-Liberalisation Era: An Inter-district and Inter-state Panel Analysis,"Economic and Political Weekly, 45, no. 20 (May 15, 2010).

[38] The Samata judgment declared null and void the transfer of land in Scheduled Areas for private mining and upheld the Forest Protection Act of 1980. See Asha Krishnakumar, "The 'Samata judgment'," Frontline, 21, no. 19, September 11-24, 2004, available online at http://www.hinduonnet.com/fline/fl2119/stories/20040924006001200.htm , accessed on July 25, 2010.

mining companies. This grabbing of tribal land also violates the Panchayat (Extension to Scheduled Areas) Act (PESA), 1996, a landmark legislation that requires consultation with *gram sabhas* before development projects in these areas can be undertaken.[39] There are scores of instances of tribal land being taken over by the State and handed over to mining companies. In Lohandiguda in Bastar, some 2,000 hectares of Fifth Schedule Area belonging to 10 villages was acquired by the government on behalf of Tata Group's Rs 1,000-crore steel plant. Tribal land in Dhurli and Bhansi villages in Dantewada district too are being acquired for the Essar Group's proposed steel plant.[40]

Economist C. P. Chandrashekar uses the term "carpetbagger capitalism" to describe the neo-liberal economic reforms that are devastating tribal areas. "Outsiders" are coming into tribal areas and reaping the profits of mining activity even as the area's indigenous inhabitants are bearing the enormous environmental, social and human costs, he says.[41] Indeed, mining activity has left tribals bearing all the costs. They are losing their land, which not only means loss of places of habitation but also their livelihood. This in turn has severely affected their access to food, water and way of life.

Tribals figure disproportionately among India's internally displaced. While they constitute 8.08 percent of India's population, they account for 40 percent of the 60 million persons displaced or affected by development

---

[39] A 45-page chapter titled "PESA, Left-Wing Extremism and Governance: Concerns and Challenges in India's Tribal Districts," which is part of a larger report commissioned by the government and researched by Institute of Rural Management, Anand (IRMA), was excluded from its final publication. The chapter provides details of how PESA is being violated in Fifth Schedule areas, providing room for the growth of left-wing extremism. See Ajay Dandekar and Chitrangada Choudhury, "PESA, Left-Wing Extremism and Governance: Concerns and Challenges in India's Tribal Districts," available online at http://www.tehelka.com/channels/ News/2010/july/10/PESAchapter.pdf, accessed on July 29, 2010.

[40] Aman Sethi, "New battle zones" Frontline, 24, no.18, Sept 8-21 2007, available online at http://www.hinduonnet.com/fline/fl2418/stories/20070921501101800.htm, accessed on September 18, 2010,

[41] C. P. Chandrashekar, "Liberalising loot,"Frontline, 27, no. 14, 3-16 July, 2010, available online at http://www.flonnet.com/fl2714/stories/20100716271400900.htm, accessed on July 15, 2010.

projects between 1947 and 2000.[42] This means that "a tribal is five times as likely as a non-tribal to be forced to sacrifice his home and hearth by the claims and demands of development and/or conservation," writes anthropologist and historian, Ramachandra Guha.[43]

In the context of the displacement caused by the Sardar Sarovar Project in western India, P Routledge has described the multiple erasures – economic, ecological and cultural - that tribals in Gujarat, Madhya Pradesh and Maharashtra have suffered.[44] In Dandakaranya too, tribals are suffering similar erasures. In 1982, when NALCO set up its bauxite extraction and refinery unit in Damanjodi in Koraput, 26 villages were affected directly and over 690 villages indirectly. Most of these were tribal villages. Several families were provided rehabilitation packages; some got financial compensation, others were provided land. NALCO officials claim that of the roughly 600 families that were displaced, 597 were provided with housing in rehabilitation colonies at Analabadi and Kontaguda. Besides, one able person from each displaced family was provided employment at NALCO.[45] Walter Fernandes, an expert on displacement, says that 60 percent of the land that was acquired by NALCO at Damanjodi was tribal common property resources and no compensation was paid for it. For the little private land they owned, tribal families were paid a paltry Rs 6,700 per hectare, "a totally inadequate sum to start a new life." [46] According to Damodar Jani, a NALCO displacee and former sarpanch of Littiguda, the land given as compensation "was uncultivable." Employment that NALCO

---

[42] Walter Fernandes, "Paying the price for someone else's displacement," InfoChange News & Features, July 2008, available online at http://infochangeindia.org/Agenda/Migration-Displacement/Paying-the-price-for-someone-else%E2%80%99s-displacement.html, accessed on July 12, 2010.

[43] Ramachandra Guha, "Adivasis, Naxalites and Indian Democracy," Economic and Political Weekly 42, no.32 (August 11-17, 2007): 3306.

[44] P Routledge, "Voices of the Dammed: Discursive Resistance amidst Erasure in the Narmada Valley, India," Political Geography, 22 (2003): 243–70.

[45] Business Standard, November 25, 2009, available online at http://www.business-standard.com/india/news/nalco-saps-at-damanjodi-demand-rr-benefits/11/22/377545/, accessed on July 12, 2010.

[46] See note 42 above.

promised the displaced "benefited only non-tribals as Adivasis were found to be lacking in the skills the company required." Some tribals got jobs but only one member per family benefited. When he died, the family was left with nothing. For most tribals, NALCO spelt economic disaster as loss of land brought loss of livelihood and sustenance to entire families.[47]

NALCO's dynamiting of the Panchapatmalli hills has destroyed the forests. Bauxite extraction dries streams. It has turned the land into a near desert making agriculture, even living there impossible. Although the NALCO factory has an ash pond and a red-mud pond, toxic effluents are being discharged into the Kolab River regularly, polluting and poisoning the water available to villages downstream.[48] Jani says that their crops and cattle are dying and the air, which is thick with flyash, is afflicting tribals with respiratory diseases.[49] This has forced tribals to move out of Damanjodi. Some have gone to Andhra Pradesh, others have moved to nearby villages around the Mali Parbat. But they will have to move soon from Mali Parbat as mining giant Hindustan Aluminum Company (HINDALCO) has acquired rights to extract bauxite from the mountain. HINDALCO is pressuring the Paroja tribe that lives in Maliguda, Tentuliguda and surrounding areas to give up land for construction of a road to the hill.[50]

Besides economic and ecological erasure, mining activity and displacement are causing erasure of tribal culture. This is the fear of the Dongria Kondh. They believe that if Niyam Dongar Hill is dynamited to facilitate bauxite extraction by UK mining giant Vedanta Resources, the home of their deity will be destroyed. The Dongria Kondhs consider the Niyam Dongar Hill to be the abode of their presiding deity, Niyam Raja (literally, the King of Law or the Universal Lawgiver). The dynamiting of their mountains will destroy their culture, their way of life, perhaps their

---

[47] Damodar Jani, interviewed by the author at Damanjodi in Orissa in December 2010.

[48] Author's observations of the Damanjodi area in December 2009.

[49] See note 47 above.

[50] See note 48 above.

survival as a distinct people.[51]

The experience of tribals living in the Chitrakonda in Malkangiri provides insights on the link between displacement, development and Maoism. Displaced by Machkund Hydel Project in Koraput back in the late 1940s, the tribals moved to Chitrakonda, only to be displaced yet again when the Balimela Hydel Project came up in 1964. Since then their villages have remained water-locked by the Chitrakonda reservoir and are accessible only by boat. No rehabilitation or socio-economic development has taken place here for decades. There are no roads, water supply or electricity. No official visits these villages. Only the Maoists bother to come to these villages and listen to the peoples' grievances. It is not surprising then that this hilly, forested region, which the rest of India has forgotten, has been a Maoist hotbed for decades.[52]

While exploitation and poverty are common themes across tribal areas, there are differences in how this exploitation takes place. In Orissa, displacement by government and private industrial and development projects has plunged tribals in poverty. In Andhra Pradesh, feudal exploitation of the landless has impoverished them. In Gadchiroli, tribals own land but those who engage in picking *tendu* leaves, cutting bamboo or collecting minor forest produce, are paid very low wages by the contractors or are harassed by forest officials.

Socio-economic indicators provide a glimpse of the impact of structural violence that tribals are subjected to. Poverty is severe and widespread

---

[51] Sudha Ramachandran, "The battle for bauxite,"Himal,Web Exclusive, August 15, 2010, available online at http://www.himalmag.com/The-battle-for-bauxite_fnw74.html, accessed on September 14, 2010. In the words of an elderly Dongria Kondh woman, "If there were no Dongria Kondh left in the hills, we wouldn't be Dongria any more as our culture and identity revolve around the mountain." "Our songs, dances, traditions are all linked to the Niyamgiri Hills. As people leave the Hills, we slowly lose our culture," another woman says. See Amnesty International, Don't mine us out of existence: Bauxite mine and refinery devastate lives in India (February 2010), 20, available online at http://www.amnesty.org/en/library/asset/ASA20/001/2010/en/0a81a1bc-f50c-4426-9505-7fde6b3382ed/asa200012010en.pdf, accessed on July 11, 2010.

[52] Author's observations of the Chitrakonda area in December 2009.

in Dandakaranya. In Dantewada, which is the epicenter of the conflict, education, health and transport infrastructure is in a shambles. Seventy-eight percent of its population is tribal. Around 52.28 percent of its people live below the poverty line and 70 percent are illiterate. Of its 1,220 villages, 1,161 have no medical facilities and 214 do not even have primary schools.[53] A similar situation of deprivation is evident in Koraput, the country's poorest district. Poverty is alarming here with four out of every five persons living below the poverty line.[54] As for Gadchiroli, more than 55 percent of its population lives below the poverty line.[55] Its child mortality rate is 144 per 1000, far higher than Maharashtra's average of 91. On the Human Development Index, the district stands last in the state. [56]

Poverty manifests itself in high rates of hunger and malnutrition, which in turn make people vulnerable to illness. It causes starvation deaths. Often hunger and starvation in tribal areas is blamed on drought or on the collapse of the public distribution system (PDS) in these areas. But the roots of the problem are more deep-seated. They lie in the structural changes that Adivasi economy has undergone over the last several decades as a result of which traditional livelihoods and food systems have been destroyed. Denied access to forests and displaced from land, their capacity to sustain their lives and livelihoods has been severely undermined.

Tribals are also victims of atrocities and rarely get justice. The police are seldom willing to register their complaints. Data compiled by the National Dalit Movement for Justice show that from 2002 to 2008, only around 20,000 cases of atrocities against tribals reached the courts every year, out of which only around 30 percent were registered under the stringent Prevention of Atrocities Act, the rest being pursued under the milder Indian Penal Code or Protection of Civil Rights Act. Around 81 percent of the cases

---

[53] 2001 Census of India figures cited in Sundar, "Bastar, Maoism and Salwa Judum," 3188.

[54] Bibek Debroy and Laveesh Bhandari, District Level Deprivation in the New Millennium (New Delhi: Konark, 2003), 26.

[55] Gadchiroli District Information, available online at http://nagpur.nicin/divisionalcommissioner/Dist_info/GAD.html, accessed on July 29, 2010.

[56] Government of India, Planning Commission, Maharashtra Development Report (New Delhi: Academic Foundation, 2007), 63 and 214.

filed by tribals are still pending.

Police harassment creates Maoists; it pushes sympathizers to go underground. In the words of a tribal in Gadchiroli, "Once there is even a minor case against you, the police arrest you every time there is a violent incident. Many Adivasis have had to sell their land or cattle to pay for the court cases against them. When they run out of money, they join the Naxalites or they go underground to escape police harassment." [57] "The police act on behalf of the exploiting class and slap us with serious charges to drive us out of our land," says Gana Nayak of Damapada village in Malkangiri district. Several in his village have been charged with sedition when all they did was protest the illegal land grabbing of tribal land by non-tribals. [58]

Acute and worsening poverty together with frustration with poor governance and the failure of the police and judiciary to deliver justice has deepened tribal alienation from the Indian State. It has encouraged tribal protest, largely democratic and peaceful but increasingly violent.

Waging Conflict

Parties to the Maoist conflict have resorted to peaceful and political means as well as coercive and violent methods. The strategy adopted depends on several factors, such as the goal, resources, the relationship between the parties, efficacy of a strategy in achieving objectives and so on. Thus for instance, the goal of overthrowing the State has determined the Maoist leadership's choice of armed struggle. For many tribals committed to peaceful means, mass struggle is preferred over ballot box politics as the latter has not delivered them results. Every party to the conflict uses a mix of methods to pursue its goals.

Tribals and Mass Protests

While the bulk of the Maoist cadres are tribal and the Maoists do enjoy some support among the tribals, armed struggle is not the dominant way in which

---

[57] Dionne Bunsha, "Guerrilla zone"Frontline, 22, no.21, Oct 8-21, 2005, available online at http://www.flonnet.com/fl2221/stories/20051021008701600.htm , accessed on July 13, 2010.

[58] Gana Nayak, interviewed by the author at Malkangiri in Orissa in December 2009.

tribals are protesting their condition. For several decades now, they have been articulating their frustration through non-violent mass protests. Since the 1970s, hundreds of tribal mass organizations have emerged to protest displacement by dams and mining projects, press for better rehabilitation and demand access to forest resources. These organizations block roads, form human chains around proposed mining sites, sit on *dharnas* (sit-ins) and go on long marches to focus attention on their grievances and pressure their adversary.

Since 1993, when the Orissa government granted a lease to Utkal Alumina International Ltd (UAIL) for extraction of bauxite from the Baphilimali hills in Kashipur, the tribal mass organization Prakrutik Sampad Suraksya Parishad (PSSP) has been protesting the bauxite mining and refining plant. The Chasi Mulia Adivasi Sangha (CMAS), which is active in Koraput, has been asserting rights over tribal land that was illegally grabbed by non-tribal landlords. For over two decades, it has been campaigning on the land issue and against consumption and sale of liquor in the area, which is a major reason for land alienation and tribal indebtedness. Among the mass organizations, the Niyamgiri Suraksha Samiti, which has been protesting Vedanta's proposed mining project at Niyamgiri, has met with some success. Its sustained campaign, which enjoyed international support, drew attention to Vedanta's violation of environmental norms, paving the way for the government refusing Vedanta permission to mine at Niyamgiri.[59]

Tribals seem to prefer mass organizational activity over ballot box politics to address their grievances. This could be because electoral politics has not benefited them much. Given their demographic distribution – tribals are concentrated in a few pockets country-wide – their capacity to influence the outcome of elections is limited. Guha points out that in parliamentary elections, for instance, the tribal vote matters in 50 to 60 constituencies, compared with around 300 constituencies in the case of Dalits.[60] Tribals are often not allowed to vote freely. Since the electoral route to shape

---

[59] Latha Jishnu, "Clampdown on Vedanta,"Down to Earth, September 15, 2010, available online at http://www.downtoearth.org.in/node/1846 ,accessed on September 18, 2010.

[60] Guha, "Adivasis, Naxalites and Indian Democracy," 3308.

government policy on issues affecting their lives has not worked for them, they prefer the other democratic option - mass mobilization and protests - to pursue their goals.

However, the appeal of armed struggle is growing.[61] The State's use of force to quell mass struggle and peaceful forms of protest, its banning of several mass organizations for their alleged links with Maoists is denying tribals the democratic avenue of protest, leaving the space open for violent waging of conflict. "We want villagers to be aware of their rights and protest peacefully if their rights are violated, not become extreme or adopt violence," a civil rights worker in Dantewada says. "But the government treats anyone who protests like an insurgent, and this only pushes people towards extremism."[62] In Orissa, Shanti Committees have been set up by landlords and mining companies and they are unleashing violence on tribals asserting their rights over land.[63] Local police support such vigilantism. This has prompted tribal youth to counter violence with violence. In these circumstances, it is not surprising that tribals are drawn to Maoist ideology and praxis and are turning to the gun to usher in a just order.

Maoists and Armed Struggle

The ultimate objective of the CPI-Maoist rebels is to capture political power through protracted 'people's war'. They do not subscribe to parliamentary politics. They believe India's democracy is a sham and that "the real

---

[61] The choice of the armed route to protest exploitation is not a recent development. Colonial expansion into tribal areas triggered armed uprisings against the British from the late 18th century onwards. The colonial administration deployed extreme force to quell these uprisings, using the Kondh practice of Mariah sacrifice as moral justification for their ruthless methods to put down the tribals. See Jaganath Pathy, "Colonial Ethnography of the Kandha: 'White Man's Burden' or Political Expediency?"Economic and Political Weekly (January 28, 1995): 220-8. While the first decade after Independence was relatively quiet in Adivasi areas, this changed from the 1960s onwards. There was a powerful uprising in the Bastar region of Chhattisgarh in 1966. The subsequent Naxalbari uprising gave a fillip to armed struggle in tribal areas in Andhra and Bihar.

[62] See note 39 above.

[63] Sudha Ramachandran, "India drives tribals into Maoist arms," Asia Times Online, January 16, 2010, available online at http://www.atimes.com/atimes/South_Asia/LA16Df03.html, accessed on July 11, 2010.

problems of the people can never be addressed by the Parliament and Assemblies, not to speak of solving them."[64] They want to overthrow the current "bourgeois order" and establish in its place a "genuine people's democracy". They believe that only systemic change can end poverty and exploitation of the poor and dispossessed and while peaceful movements through mass protests can usher in regime change, these cannot bring systemic change. "A section of the ruling classes might give up power to another section of the same class without the need for a violent upheaval but the same is not the case when one ruling class is replaced by another with diametrically opposing class interests," 'Azad', the recently slain former spokesperson of the Maoists said. Since systemic change is their goal, Maoists believe that this necessitates armed struggle.[65]

Besides armed struggle, the Maoists engage in political work among the tribals, which includes their indoctrination in Maoist ideology and strategy but also development work in the villages.[66] In areas under their control, Naxalites are said to be running *janatana sarkars* or 'parallel governments'. They hold *jan adalats* (informal public courts) that dispense quick and often ruthless justice. They take up development activities, such as digging wells and canals and put pressure on State functionaries to perform better.

Maoists say they have taken up armed struggle to overthrow the State and put in its place an egalitarian system, one that will provide India's poorest and most marginalized sections with distributive justice. It is not surprising then that their call to arms strikes a chord with tribals and other dispossessed communities.

---

[64] Comrade Ganapathy, "Interview with Comrade Ganapathy," Revolution in South Asia: An Internationalist Info Project, available online at http://southasiarev.wordpress.com/nepal-worker-11/the-worker-11-interview-with-com-ganapathy/, accessed on July 21, 2010.

[65] Ibid.

[66] The Maoists first identify the local grievances – genuine and perceived, then work on drawing attention of the people to government policies that underlie their poverty and problems, and on convincing them that working with the Moaists will end their exploitation. Once they have local support, they work on weakening the structures of civil governance and through a systematic campaign of threats and terror, remove representatives of the State that are opposed to them. They infiltrate local representative bodies. Their objective is to throw out State institutions from the area so that they can occupy the political space and set up their janatana sarkar.

State Response to Tribal Alienation and Maoist Violence

What is the government's strategy to tackle tribal alienation and Maoism? Over the decades, the government has adopted a multi-pronged approach to deal with the Maoist conflict. To address tribal grievances that underlie their growing alienation from the State and consequent support for the Maoists, it has implemented an array of poverty alleviation programs and enacted legislation to protect tribal rights and interests.[67] To deal with the Maoists, it has pursued negotiations, albeit half-heartedly, even as its strategy has focused on military operations against them.

The Fifth Schedule of the Indian Constitution designates districts in nine states as tribal areas. Most of the land in the districts that fall under the Dandakaranya region are Fifth Schedule Areas. The Fifth Schedule guarantees tribals rights over the land they live in. It gives governors of the states in question extensive powers to prevent or amend any law enacted in the parliament or the state assembly that could harm tribals' interests. PESA, which was enacted in 1996, goes further to protect tribal rights by providing for tribal self-governance and recognizing the traditional rights of tribal communities over their natural resources. PESA provides for the setting up of *gram sabhas* and *gram panchayats* to enable tribals to take control of their destinies. It empowers them to protect community resources, control social sector functionaries, own minor forest produce, manage water bodies, give recommendations for mining lease, be consulted for land acquisition, enforce prohibition, identify beneficiaries for poverty alleviation and other government programs, and have a decisive say in all development projects in the villages.[68]

---

[67] For an overview of constitutional/legislative safeguards and developmental programs and measures adopted by the government, see Ram Babu Mallavarapu, "Development, Displacement and Rehabilitation: An Action Anthropological Study on Kovvada Reservoir in West Godavari Agency of Andhra Pradesh, India," International Journal of Social Sciences, 1, no. 1 (Winter 2006), available online at http://www.waset.org/journals/ijss/v1/v1-1-7.pdf, accessed on July 11, 2010.

[68] Vidhya Das, "PESA: A Reality Check,"Agragamee, available online at http://www.agragamee.org/newinitiatives_pesa.htm, accessed on July 5, 2010.

Besides, the government has taken steps to strengthen the livelihood security of tribals and other rural poor through the Mahatma Gandhi National Rural Employment Guarantee Act (MGNREGA), 2005, and the more tribal-specific Scheduled Tribes and Other Traditional Forest Dwellers (Recognition of Forest Rights) Act, 2006, better known as the Forest Rights Act (FRA). MGNREGA guarantees a hundred days of wage employment in a year to a rural household. Manual work carried out under MNREGA not only provides jobs and wages but also, it contributes to building economic and social infrastructure in rural areas. As for the FRA, this landmark legislation recognizes the forest rights of tribal communities, including the right to live in the forest, to self-cultivate, and to use minor forest produce. It empowers the *gram sabha* to initiate the process of determining the extent of forest rights that may be given to each eligible individual or family and gives forest communities primacy in forest management.

In the wake of growing protest over land acquisition and consequent displacement, the government has formulated the National Rehabilitation & Resettlement Policy, 2007. The stated aim of the policy is striking "a balance between the need for land for developmental activities and, at the same time, protecting the interests of the land owners, and others.... whose livelihood depends on the land involved." It seeks to minimize displacement and to promote, "as far as possible, non-displacing or least-displacing alternatives; to ensure adequate rehabilitation package and expeditious implementation of the rehabilitation process with the active participation of the affected families; to ensure that special care is taken for protecting the rights of the weaker sections especially members of tribal and Dalit communities." In the event of a large number of families being affected, the policy makes mandatory social impact assessments and provision of infrastructure and amenities in the resettlement areas. Where tribals "are being displaced in sizeable numbers, a well thought out Tribal Development Plan must be put in place," the policy says. [69]

---

[69] For text of the policy see, Government of India, Ministry of Rural Development, National Rehabilitation and Resettlement Policy, 2007, available online at http://www. indiaenvironmentportal.org.in/files/NRRP2007.pdf, accessed on July 6, 2010.

To reduce the crushing impact of poverty, the government has implemented several programs aimed at reducing hunger and malnutrition, improving literacy and so on. The Integrated Child Development Scheme (ICDS), for instance, aims at ensuring food and health security of children under the age of six years. The PDS aims at providing those below the poverty line with food grains at subsidized rates. Tribal children are among those groups that are the prime focus of the Sarva Shiksha Abhiyan, a literacy program that aims at achieving universal elementary education through opening new schools in areas that do not have schooling facilities, strengthening existing school infrastructure and so on.

An important component of the government's approach to development of tribal areas is to encourage investment in the extraction and refining of the immense mineral wealth of the Dandakaranya region, the argument being that this 'development' will provide tribals with jobs, even as it spurs India's economic growth. As discussed earlier, extraction and refining of minerals was the prerogative of the government up to the 1990s. Since liberalization of the economy, a number of private companies, Indian and multi-national, have entered tribal areas.

Besides seeking to address tribal poverty and discontent in a bid to reduce their alienation with the Indian State and to draw them away from the Maoists, the government is also taking steps to tackle the Maoists. The Andhra Pradesh government, for instance, engaged in talks with the Maoists in 2004. The peace process collapsed within a few months.

The government has also used the legislative route to tackle the Maoists. On June 22, 2009, the CPI (Maoist) was listed as a terrorist organization under the Unlawful Activities (Prevention) Act (UAPA). The CPI (Maoist)'s naming in the list made little difference on the ground as the ban on the organization was already in effect by virtue of the fact that its constituents, the PWG, MCC and their front organizations were already outlawed under the UAPA and its earlier incarnation, the Prevention of Terrorism Act (POTA). Barring brief periods in 1995 and 2004-05 when the ban on it was lifted, the PWG has functioned as an outlawed group for much of the time since it was first banned in 1992 in Andhra. Several suspected front organizations of the Maoists have also been banned.

The government's approach to tackling the Maoists has leaned on coercive means. Right from the 1940s, it has used extreme force to suppress the Maoists. As discussed in an earlier section, the scale and nature of anti-Maoist operations have escalated over the decades. Besides police and paramilitary forces, special commando units are being deployed in districts worst hit by Maoist violence. Use of extra-legal groups like Salwa Judum has been an important part of the government's strategy.

Since 2009, the Centre has been working on a two-pronged strategy that includes coordinated military operations to eliminate Maoists from districts that are the worst affected by Maoist violence, followed by developmental activity. A senior Home Ministry official has described this as "a comprehensive operational strategy that would first seek to clear an area of Maoists, occupy it militarily and follow it up with socio-economic development activity."[70] In a statement in Parliament, Home Minister P. Chidambaram said that "the two pillars of the policy are calibrated police action and development. Central paramilitary forces have been provided to the affected states, including Chhattisgarh, to help the state governments carry out counter-insurgency operations, regain control of areas dominated by the Naxalites, restore the civil administration, and restart development work."[71] While the government has described its policy towards Maoists as one that is as much about development as it is about elimination of Maoists, it is clearly more preoccupied with the latter at present. Some have drawn parallels between the violence of the Salwa Judum strategy and that of Operation Green Hunt, the only difference being that "Operation Green Hunt is being conducted under the official mandate of the State, rather than under the fig leaf of a so-called 'people's movement'."[72]

Security analysts have often argued that the government has been compelled to use military means against the Maoists as the political and

---

[70] Venkitesh Ramakrishnan, "Flawed operation," Frontline, 27, no. 9, April 9 May 24, 2009, available online at http://flonnet.com/fl2709/stories/20100507270900400.htm , accessed on July 11, 2010.

[71] Ibid.

[72] Nandini Sundar, "Pleading for Justice," Seminar, 607, March 2010, available online at http://www.india-seminar.com/2010/607/607_nandini_sundar.htm, accessed on July 11, 2010.

constitutional means have not worked with them. They often point to the failed talks in 2004-05 to allege that the Maoists used this period to regroup rather than find a negotiated solution. However, a close examination of how events unfolded during this period reveals that negotiations failed because they were not pursued by either side seriously or in a way that would result in a constructive outcome.[73] Furthermore, while the government has put in place several projects to address poverty and hunger in tribal areas, implementation of these has been half-hearted. Funds have benefited contractors and middlemen rather than the tribals. Besides, the government's approach to economic development of tribal areas, which consists of encouraging investment in mining and other extractive activity, is deepening structural violence and inequity.

Thus, while the main parties are using a range of political, legislative, developmental and military measures to pursue their goals, they have pursued the political and constitutional means less assiduously than they have the military ones. What is the impact of the violent waging of conflict? The following paragraphs turn to this examination.

Impact of the Maoist Conflict

The previous section explored the various ways in which the conflict is being waged. It drew attention to the predominantly violent way that it is being waged. An important point that was discussed is the State's use of illegal violence and its violation of the Constitution. What have been its consequences for India's democracy? What has been the impact of the armed conflict on people living there? What kind of governance have Maoists provided in areas under their control? This section will explore some of these questions.

Spiral of Violence

Experience in armed conflicts across the world indicates that violence that is employed to quell violence often intensifies it. Attacks trigger counter-attacks and each violent action prompts a reaction that is more severe. Each

---

[73] K Balagopal, "Naxalites in Andhra Pradesh: Have We Heard the Last of the Peace Talks?"Economic and Political Weekly, 40, no 13 (March 26-April 1, 2005): 1323-9.

side aggresses against the other in response to the other's hostility. This results in a spiral of violence. Such spirals are fed by movement from light to heavier tactics.

The Maoist conflict is caught in a spiral of violence. An attack by one side prompts retaliation by the other. Such retaliation by the security forces, for instance, takes the form of not just intensified search operations to hunt out Maoists but collective punishment that is meted out to villagers who are thought to have supported the rebels. This is turn triggers a heavier Maoist response. With both sides engaging in punishment and revenge, each is seeking to retaliate with deadlier violence. Not only is the level of violence intensifying but also the list of grievances and issues of conflict are growing.

The Maoists claim that their ambush of CRPF personnel at Chintalnar in April 2010 was in response to the government's bid to reclaim areas they controlled for years. The Chintalnar ambush became the harbinger of more violence and bloodletting. Fearing police wrath and reprisals, hundreds of tribals from the surrounding villages of Mukram, Tarmetla, Rehadgatta, Pamra, Karigundam, Kodapalli, Rengam, Murpalli and Jadka fled to neighboring Orissa and Andhra Pradesh. Those who stayed back have had to bear the brunt of police intimidation and/or Maoist punishment. The village of Mukram has been the worst affected. One of the Maoist commanders, Rukhmati, who participated in the ambush, was from this village and it was in Mukram that the CRPF personnel rested the night before the ambush. For these 'links' with the Maoists, Mukram's residents have become the focus of its search operations and the target of the punishment being meted out by the CRPF. Aimla Rane, wife of Mukram's *sarpanch,* says that the CRPF spared no one in her village. They "beat every man, woman and child they could find and they took away my husband, Aimla Nanda," she recalls. The CRPF has reportedly detained him and several others in its camp at Chintalnar. Girls from the village are alleged to have been raped at the CRPF camp nearby. Not surprisingly, Mukram is "turning into a ghost village."[74]

---

[74] The Hindu, May 29, 2010, available online at http://beta.thehindu.com/news/states/other-states/article440889.ece, accessed on July 12, 2010.

This is a brief summary of what Mukram's residents have suffered over a few weeks. For those living in zones of armed conflict like Dantewada, this cycle of violence is a familiar experience. An attack or offensive by one side leads to reprisals by the other, which in turn prompts more intimidation, punishment and violence.

Human Costs of the Conflict

Ordinary civilians are getting caught in the crossfire between the security forces and the Maoists. The experience of Shyamal Pojamma, a resident of Koras village in Chhattisgarh, provides insights into the multiple implications that conflict has for people living in the conflict zone. They suffer the impact of loss of kin, trauma and the unending pain of displacement. Pojammma fled to Andhra Pradesh to escape the Salwa Judum. But insecurity dogs her. Here is her account:

> *My 18-year old son, Shyamal Admaiya, was killed by the Salwa Judum and the police in a fake encounter in Singaram village on January 8, 2009. I saw his body. He was shot between the eyes. In addition to this, they had used a sickle to cut open his head. I can't erase the images from my mind. Admaiya was my youngest son.*
>
> *For two months after this, we lived in the forest, terrified that the Salwa Judum would come back and kill the rest of us. My two older sons and their families decided to walk to Andhra Pradesh since they were tired of constantly living in fear. I refused to leave. I wanted to die in my village. If I left, there would be nobody to remember the place where my son was killed.*
>
> *Two weeks ago, the Salwa Judum returned to my village. My husband and I escaped again to the forest. When my two sons heard of this, they came to the village and brought us here. We walked for an entire day but that is of no consequence. If I could bring back Admaiya, I would walk for a year.*

There is no food here, no lands to cultivate. For me, this is
alien land since none of my ancestors are buried here. Come back
and talk to me in a year and I will tell you so even then. Back
home we were kings. Now all we can afford is one portion of rice
gruel a day. The Naxals are safe, the Salwa Judum is safe. We are
the only ones dying in the middle.[75]

Pojamma's experience of the conflict is not an isolated one. Many tribals in Chhattisgarh have undergone similar tragedies. The death of loved ones, dealing with trauma and 'disappearances', shattered livelihoods, displacement – these are just a few ways in which armed conflict devastates people's lives. Combatants – whether Maoist or security forces - and their families too pay a heavy price. If caught by the adversary, combatants are often tortured, even executed. The homes of Maoist fighters are routinely searched and ransacked by the security forces. The families are tortured for information.

There are innumerable allegations of rape and 'disappearance' of civilians in the conflict zone. "Those who participate in protests over land are 'disappearing'," says a Koya youth in Tentuliguda in Malkangiri, referring to 50-year-old Indromadi who went missing in August 2008. Indromadi was part of the Malkangiri Zilla Adivasi Sangha and following up on the disappearance of another person from the village.[76]

The armed conflict has left thousands dead. With the main adversaries opting for military means, the number of fatalities has grown sharply over the years, particularly in the current phase of escalation. Table 2 indicates that the number of fatalities has almost doubled between 2002 and 2009.

---

[75] Shyamal Pojamma, 'We are the only ones dying," Tehelka, 7, no. 6, February 13, 2010, available online at http://www.tehelka.comstory_main43.asp? filename =Ne130210JT08. asp, accessed on July 14, 2010.

[76] Koya youth interviewed by the author at Tentuliguda in Orissa in December 2009.

Table 2: Number of Fatalities in the Maoist Conflict, 2002-2009

Year	2002	2003	2004	2005	2006	2007	2008	2009
Number of Fatalities	482	515	566	677	678	696	721	908

Source: Government of India, Ministry of Home Affairs, *Annual Report, 2005-06; Annual Report, 2008-09; Annual Report, 2009-10.*

The number injured is far higher; many are dealing with lifelong physical disabilities, and mental and psychological conditions. The Maoists' increasing use of improvised explosive devices (IEDs) is taking a heavy toll on the security forces. IEDs account for about 40 percent of the 408 troop fatalities in Chhattisgarh since 2007 and nearly 70 percent of all injuries sustained by security forces from January 2008 to March 2010. IEDs cause death and injuries. Their psychological impact is devastating.[77]

With the main adversaries adopting tactics that result in civilian casualties, an increasing number of civilians are being killed in the conflict. Civil liberties and rights organizations have long alleged that many of so-called 'Maoists' the police claim to have eliminated are in fact innocent civilians.[78]

In October 2009, 11 Adivasis of Gompad village in Chhattisgarh were killed by a composite force including SPOs and police. The area is one that is frequented by Maoists and security forces but those who were killed in the massacre were civilians.[79] Madivi Muthi, who lost several members of her family in that killing, recalls:

---

[77] Aman Sethi, "Troop fatality figures show changing Maoist strategy," The Hindu, April 5, 2010, available online at http://www.hindu.com/2010/04/05/stories/2010040554290900.htm, accessed on July 14, 2010.

[78] Shivam Vij, "Vigilante State," Tehelka, June 2, 2007, available online at http://www.tehelka.com/story_main30.asp?filename=Ne020607Vigilante_state_SR.asp, accessed on September 14, 2010.

[79] The Hindu, Feb 21, 2010, available online at http://beta.thehindu.com/news/national/article110448.ece, accessed on July11, 2010.

The men either shot them [those who stayed back in the village when the attack happened] or hacked them down - inside their houses. I lost my uncle, Madivi Bajar, my aunt, Madivi Subbi and another family member, Madivi Venkaiah. Two others in the village, Soyan Subbaiah and Soyan Jogi, were also killed. The men looted their house as well – I heard that they took away all the money in the house. I don't know if the men who attacked our village were people from the Salwa Judum or the police.... I was told that the police claim that the people who were killed in Gompad were Naxals. The people they killed were not Naxals - they lived in our village. I knew them my entire life. They killed innocent people sleeping in their houses and called them Naxals. Were they afraid to catch the real ones?[80]

Often it is civilians who bear the brunt of Maoist attacks, even those that target the security forces. The Maoists attack the security forces, then melt into the forests and leave civilians to face the ire of the security forces. Many civilians have faced the wrath of the Maoists and the security forces. Aimla Nanda, who has been in CRPF custody since the Chintalnar ambush was the target of Maoist ire in 2004. He was tied to a tree for criticizing their destruction of a village school.[81]

The impact of the conflict has been particularly harsh on children. Children's education has been severely affected as many schools have been occupied by the security forces. Maoists too have blown up several schools.[82]

More worrying is the recruitment of children by the State, the Salwa Judum and the Maoists in Chhattisgarh. The Maoists organize children in

---

[80] Madivi Muthi, "Those killed were not Naxals," Tehelka, 7, no. 6, February 13, 2010, available online at http://www.tehelka.comstory_main43.asp?filename= Ne130210JT07. asp, accessed on July 11, 2010.

[81] The Hindu, May 29, 2010, available online at http://beta.thehindu.com/news/states/other-states/article440889.ece, accessed on July 11, 2010.

[82] Human Rights Watch, Sabotaged Schooling: Naxalite Attacks and Police Occupation of Schools in India's Bihar and Jharkhand States (New York: HRW 2009).

the 6-12 age group into *bal sanghams*, where they are indoctrinated on Maoist ideology and prepared for later *dalam* activity. Those above 12 years of age are deployed as fighters, to engage in hostilities against the security forces and the Salwa Judum, to make and plant landmines and bombs, to gather intelligence and for sentry duty. Children have been recruited by the Salwa Judum for similar purposes. What is more, the State is recruiting children as SPOs. [83]

Tarrem Kosa's experience as a child soldier with the Maoists and then as an SPO lays bare the tragic lives of children living in the conflict zone. A student of class eight when he was recruited into a Maoist *dalam*, Tarrem Kosa was trained with bows and arrows, then bombs. He participated in several encounters. Recalling his years in a *dalam* he says: "I used to think of home a lot. I worried I would never be able to contact my parents. I used to read magazines to kill time ... Sometimes I would sit and cry. I never had the opportunity to contact my parents. I thought of home a lot, but never had a way to get back." He paid a heavy price when he left the Maoists. They killed both his younger brothers, beat his mother and broke her arm, took all their belongings, and burned their house. After his surrender to the police – he was not an adult then - Tarrem Kosa began to work for them as an informer, and then became an SPO. He now accompanies security forces on anti-Maoist combing operations. He is wanted by the Maoists and says he has seen posters with his photograph that say he should be killed.[84] For many in the conflict zone - civilians or combatants - there appears to be no escape from a life of violence.

Geographical Expansion of Conflict

There has been a phenomenal expansion in the area of Maoist activity over the decades and especially over the past decade. In the early 1990s, 15 districts in four states were reported to be affected by Maoist violence. In November 2003, 55 districts of nine states were described as 'Maoist-affected'. The figure jumped to 156 districts in 13 states within ten months.

---

[83] Human Rights Watch, Dangerous Duty: Children and the Chhattisgarh Conflict (New York: HRW, 2008).

[84] Ibid., 31-32.

In September 2009, Home Minister Chidambaram said that 223 districts across 20 states (of a total 626 districts and 28 states) were hit by Maoist activity. Terrorism analyst Ajai Sahni argues that areas of 'Maoist activity' or those that are 'Maoist-affected' include not only areas hit by violence but also those that are in "the early stages of 'revolutionary mobilization' - the creation of basic networks, the establishment of underground and 'overground' organizations, and the opportunistic harnessing of local grievances for radical political activity." Thus, not all the 223 districts are convulsed in violence. However, the Home Minister also disclosed that violence "has been consistently witnessed in about 400 police station areas of around 90 districts in 13 states." Ninety districts experiencing consistent violence is "by far greater than the total of 55 variously affected districts in 2003," Sahni points out.[85] The present decade has witnessed not only an expansion in the area of Maoist influence and activity of varying degrees but in the area experiencing consistent violence.

The expansion of areas of consistent violence is the result of both the Maoists' expansion strategy and the State's military operations. Anti-Maoist operations by the Greyhounds, a special anti-Maoist unit, in Andhra Pradesh since the 1990s forced hundreds of Maoist fighters to escape to 'safe havens' in the Dandakaranya forests of neighboring Chhattisgarh, Orissa and Maharashtra. Chhattisgarh was an area of low-key Maoist activity in the 1990s and Maoist attacks consisted of strikes on police outposts in remote areas. The flight of Maoists from Andhra made it the prime focus of Maoist attention from the late 1990s. Its emergence as the epicenter of the conflict is as much the result of the Salwa Judum as it is of Greyhound operations in Andhra. Besides, the government's strategy of arming villagers to 'defend themselves' against the Maoists is being implemented in more areas. This is drawing more areas into the zone of violent conflict.

Breakdown of Rule of Law

A breakdown of the rule of law is evident across large stretches of territory that are roiled in violence and conflict. This breakdown is as much the

---

[85] Ajai Sahni, "The Dreamscape of 'Solutions'," Seminar, 607, March 2010, available online at http://www.india-seminar.com/semsearch.htm, accessed on July 11, 2010.

outcome of Maoist activity as it is of the State and its functionaries. In areas under Maoist control it is Maoist 'laws', not those laid down by the Indian Constitution that are in effect. It is often reported that in districts like Malkangiri, tribal mass organizations and Maoists are grabbing land illegally and taking the law into their hands. Indeed, these organizations have taken control of thousands of acres of agricultural land from non-tribals. However, more often than not they are wresting control of land that is theirs under Indian laws. As discussed earlier, land in Fifth Schedule areas is recognized as tribal land and its alienation to non-tribals is illegal. If tribals are 'grabbing land' they are doing so to take back what belongs to them. They are asserting their constitutional rights. Tribal activists say that with the police and courts supporting non-tribals, they have been pushed to take the law into their hands to enforce what is due to them under the Constitution and various legislations.[86]

Officials help non-tribals take possession of tribal land. They are aiding the violating of laws. Worse, the State is itself showing scant regard for laws. Legislations like PESA have been "observed in the breach by the state governments" that govern Fifth Schedule areas.[87] The laws enacted by state governments to implement PESA militate against its spirit.

The State's acquisition of tribal land for development and mining activity is a gross violation of laws it has formulated. Under PESA, the State cannot acquire land or issue mining rights on tribal lands without the permission of the *gram sabha*. However, state functionaries are acquiring tribal land, ignoring the opposition of *gram sabhas*. There have been many instances of police intimidating *gram sabhas* to give their consent. This was the case with land acquisition by the Tata Group and Essar Steel in Chhattisgarh. In 2006, the villages of Sirisguda, Belar, Takraguda, Kumli, Dhuragaon, Chindgaon, Bhadeparoda and Dabpal in Bastar were subjected to repeated pressure from police and civil administration officials to compel

---

[86] Tribal activists interviewed by the author in Malkangiri in Orissa in December 2009.

[87] Mani Shankar Aiyar, "Government's sheathed weapon," Economic Times, May 20, 2010, available at http://economictimes.indiatimes.com/articleshow/5951556.cms, accessed on July 4, 2010.

them to hand over their land to Tata's steel project in Bastar. Officials imposed ban orders and tight security cordons around the venue of *gram sabha* meetings. Hundreds of police were deployed in the area to intimidate the tribals, even as administration and company officials pressured *gram sabha* members to agree to hand over their land.[88]

In Andhra Pradesh, work on the Polavaram dam project across the River Godavari is going on despite the opposition of tribals. The project is located in Fifth Schedule area and will displace at a minimum around 276 villages, all them situated in Fifth Schedule area. Under PESA, *gram sabhas* have to be consulted but not one of the nine *mandal praja parishads,* which are the "panchayat of the appropriate level" that should be consulted under PESA rules, has been consulted. Yet the project is steaming ahead.[89]

The violation of the Constitution by the State, the intervention of the State on behalf of private business interests and its nurturing of vigilante groups have undermined the credibility of the Indian Constitution. The State cannot absolve itself of responsibility for the breakdown of law and order in the tribal areas as it is the "principal violator of the very laws it is meant to uphold."[90]

Civil War Situation

More disturbing is the use of extra-judicial violence by the State. Captured Maoists are executed instead of putting them through the due process of justice. They are eliminated in fake encounters.[91] In Andhra Pradesh, the police armed surrendered Maoists not only to fight the Maoists but also eliminate civil society activists who were critical of the police. Killer gangs with names like Nallamalla Black Cobras, Kakatiya Cobras, Naxalite

---

[88] See note 40 above.

[89] K. Balagopal, "Illegal Acquisition in Tribal Areas "Economic and Political Weekly, 42, no. 40 (October 6 - 2, 2007): 4003.

[90] See note 39 above.

[91] Maoist leader 'Azad' was reportedly shot at point-blank range indicating that he was executed rather than killed in an encounter. Anuradha Raman and Saikat Datta, "Shoot and Shut Up,"Outlook, September 13, 2010, available online at http://www.outlookindia.com/article.aspx?266974 , accessed on September 18, 2010.

Victims Association and Narsa Cobras that targeted dozens of human rights activists were nurtured by the police.[92]

The State took its extra-legal violence to a new level through the setting up of the Salwa Judum and the arming of tribals in the name of fighting Maoists. This has militarized society. Salwa Judum has divided tribal society into pro-Maoist and anti-Maoist villages. It has turned brother against brother, and village against village. It has pitted tribal society against itself. Salwa Judum has turned the conflict in Dantewada into a near civil war.

When it was set up, tribals were forced to attend Salwa Judum rallies, express support for the Salwa Judum and oppose the Maoists. Many village heads, whose authority was usurped by *sangham* leaders, saw Salwa Judum as an opportunity to wrest back their lost power. They decided on behalf of their villages to support the Salwa Judum. Those who refused were killed. Villages that refused to join the Salwa Judum were deemed 'Maoist villages' and attacked. Entire villages were burned down. Over 600 villages were thus emptied out and the land then became 'Salwa Judum land,' which was sold to mining companies and other vested interests. Land which wasn't under Salwa Judum control was looked upon as 'Maoist land' and blockaded. Thus Salwa Judum divided the people and the land. There was no scope for neutrality in this war. Villagers could not anymore remain aloof from the fighting.

Researcher Jason Miklian has described how Salwa Judum has "altered the conflict landscape in Dantewada." He says that Salwa Judum has resulted in "warlordization of the region." Local Salwa Judum leaders control the relief camps set up for the displaced. They 'protect' them from the Maoists and in return receive funding, food and weapons from the Chhattisgarh government. "The leaders meet monthly to demarcate Dantewada territory among themselves, consolidate efforts to increase monetary and arms support from the state, and strategically plan to ensure that Salwa Judum

[92] P. C. Vinoj Kumar, "The Cobra Fields," Tehelka, March 4, 2006, available online at http://www.tehelka.comstory_main16.asp?filename= Ne030406The_cobra_SR.asp, accessed on July 10, 2010.

continues to thrive." Increasingly, the Salwa Judum warlords seem to be functioning autonomously. It is the Salwa Judum warlords and camp leaders who 'police' roads in parts of Dantewada and stop and search vehicles plying on 'their territory.' It is the Salwa Judum, not the police - not even its higher echelons - that call the shots in places like Dornapal, Miklian points out.[93]

Whatever authority the government exercised over the villages and small towns in Dantewada seem to have been ceded to the Salwa Judum.

Displacement

The violent conflict and especially the Salwa Judum have triggered an exodus of tribals from the conflict zone. The Salwa Judum alone is said to have displaced people from around 600 villages in south Chhattisgarh. Caught in the violence and counter-violence of the Salwa Judum and the Maoists, thousands of tribals fled their homes. The Salwa Judum is reported to have forced tribals to leave their villages. Some of them were sent to relief camps run by the Salwa Judum. Others fled to neighboring Andhra and Orissa. Those who stayed back in the villages or escaped to the forests were labeled Maoists and attacked.

Life in the camps has not been easy. Tribals living here were held as virtual prisoners and not allowed to return to their homes or to cultivate their land. They, including children, have been recruited into the Salwa Judum.[94] In 2008, the NHRC reported that those in the relief camps were "the leaders/activists of Salwa Judum, ordinary villagers who support Salwa Judum, and SPO's family members." [95]

Those who returned to their villages have not been provided rehabilitation support. "Affected villagers have no access to health care, government services, or markets to buy and sell goods. These villages have no PDS, handpumps, schools, health workers or *anganwadi* [government-run child care centers to address malnutrition] workers, and the administration

---

[93] Miklian, "The Purification Hunt,"449-50.

[94] Ibid., 451

[95] See note 72 above.

has completely withdrawn from the area. These services have been diverted to the camps." By denying villagers basic facilities and diverting these to the camps, "the government is providing rehabilitation only to Salwa Judum members and SPOs and not to victims of Salwa Judum."[96]

As for those who've crossed to neighboring states, they are "eking a living on the margins of existence."[97] Although the areas they have fled to like Khammam and Malkangiri are Fifth Schedule areas, the displaced tribal groups are not always classified as Scheduled Tribes (STs) in the host state. Thus, while Telugu-speaking Koyas such as the Dora Koya have ST status in Andhra, the Gondi-speaking Gothikoyas are not recognized as STs here. Displacement to Andhra deprives the Gothikoyas of their ST entitlements.[98] Moreover, they are denied even their entitlements under the PDS or the MGNREGA, as they do not originally belong to the state. They are treated "as non-citizens at best, or Maoist supporters at worst". [99]

Gothikoya tribals fleeing Salwa Judum and Maoist terror in Dantewada continue to live in terror in Khammam. The tribals have put up huts in the forests here and have been careful not to cultivate land. Still their huts and belongings are burnt by forest department officials. "The forest officials of Khammam district attack our makeshift dwellings in the forests asking us to vacate the forest land. With cops, Salwa Judum men targeting us on one side and Maoists on the other, we are caught in a no man's land," Madakam Bira, a tribal from Kunta area, said.[100] Sarivela-Kothuru and Sunnam Matka are among the habitations that have been set on fire several times by the officials. [101]

---

[96] Ibid.

[97] See note 39 above.

[98] Bert Suykens, "'You know we are Indians too'," The Newsletter, no. 53 (Spring 2010), available online at http://213.207.98.211/files/IIAS_NL53_19.pdf, accessed on July 6, 2010.

[99] See note 39 above.

[100] Times of India November 11, 2009, available online at http://timesofindia.indiatimes.com/city/hyderabad/Tribal-influx-on-the-rise-in-Khammam/articleshow/5217384.cms, accessed on July 15, 2010.

[101] Balagopal, "Illegal Acquistions,"4033.

Khammam district alone has an estimated 16,024 displaced living in some 203 settlements. Besides the violence of the Salwa Judum, the Maoists and forest officials, there is the conflict over scarce resources between villages. This has manifested itself in more violence for the tribals. Ramachandrapuram was attacked by the Maoists. Soon after, its residents gave the police an erroneous tip-off that led to the latter killing one tribal and arresting two others from Kamantome on the suspicion that they are Maoists. While the two were subsequently freed, they remain traumatized. Madvi Hidme recalls how after tying his hands behind his back, police hung him from the ceiling and interrogated him at the Bhadrachalam police station.[102]

Hunger, malnutrition and water scarcity are rampant among the displaced in Andhra. Sociologist Nandini Sundar describes their condition as "alarming". A survey of 482 children in refugee settlements conducted by NGOs in Andhra revealed that 76.6 percent of them are in various stages of malnutrition with 27.2 percent suffering from third grade or severe malnutrition.[103] Diseases like malaria, diarrhea and cholera, always rampant in these jungle areas, have increased in intensity in the settlements for the displaced. Lack of access to drinking water has triggered outbreaks of epidemics like scabies.[104]

Democracy Undermined

The State claims to be fighting the Maoists in defense of India's parliamentary democracy and the Maoists say their goal is to replace India's sham democracy with a genuine democracy, a people's democracy. Yet experience on the ground shows that the actions of both adversaries has weakened democracy.

The State is criminalizing dissent. Critics of its counterinsurgency

---

[102] Javed Iqbal, "The Starving Guests of Khammam," New Indian Express, 6 June 2010, available online at http://expressbuzz.com/search/the-starving-guests-of-khammam/178986.html, accessed on July 21, 2010.

[103] See note 72 above.

[104] Kristin Elizabeth Solberg, " Health Crisis amid the Maoist Insurgency in India," The Lancet, 371, no. 9261, April 19, 2008, available online at http://www.thelancet.com/journals/lancet/article/PIIS0140-6736(08)60577-2/fulltext, accessed on July 14, 2010.

policy are dubbed as Maoist. In fact, in the conflict zone any protest or criticism of government actions is labeled 'Maoist'. "We protest about anything – the corruption in NREGA, the takeover of our land, and we are immediately dubbed Maoist," a sarpanch in Koraput says. "Basically, if we raise our voice against something the government is doing, no matter how illegal or unfair we feel it might be to us, we become Naxals and Maoists."[105] Those who work amidst tribals are also labeled Maoist. This was the fate of Binayak Sen, a doctor cum civil rights activist, who was in custody for two years before he was let out on bail.[106] A health worker who used to visit villages of the Bonda tribe in Malkangiri "where no government doctor, nurse or government official would ever care to go," received a letter from the Collector ordering her to leave the district. The reason behind the order was that since she was working in villages in the Maoist zone, she "must be a Maoist." [107]

In May 2010, the Home Ministry warned civil society groups, NGOs, intellectuals and the general public that supporting the Maoist ideology would attract action under UAPA. [108] It has drawn up a list of 57 organizations it says are working "for the cause of the Maoists". While some of the organizations in this list do indeed have Maoist links, many do not. Organizations like the People's Union for Civil Liberties (PUCL) and the People's Union for Democratic Rights (PUDR) that figure in the list have condemned the State's use of extrajudicial methods even as they are critical of human rights violations by Maoists. Several of the listed organizations engage in democratic activity in the public domain, even contesting elections. Rights activists have pointed out that the government's definition of a rebel sympathizer is so "open-ended", that "anyone working

---

[105] See note 39 above.

[106] Shoma Choudhury, "The Doctor, the State and, a Sinister Case," Tehelka, 5, no. 7, February 23, 2008, available online at http://www.tehelka.com/story_main37.asp?filename=Ne230208The_Doctor.asp, accessed on July 30, 2010.

[107] See note 39 above.

[108] Sudha Ramachandran, "Delhi targets rebels with a cause," Asia Times Online, June 8, 2010, available online at http://www.atimes.com/atimes/South_Asia/LF08Df01.html, accessed on July 30, 2010.

for tribal rights will get branded as pro-Maoist".[109]

Several draconian laws aid the State in its undermining of democracy. These include the UAPA and the Chhattisgarh Special Public Security Act (CSPSA), 2005, which empower police to arrest anyone without hard evidence and imprison him without due process. In the name of fighting Maoists the CSPSA has led to increased repression and suppression of people's rights. It criminalizes even peaceful protest, declaring it "a danger or menace to public order, peace and tranquility" because it might interfere with or "tends to interfere with the maintenance of public order [or] the administration of law."[110]

The Maoists display a similar "if you are not for us, you are against us" perception of the world. In response to a 2006 letter by the Independent Citizens Initiative (ICI) calling on the government and the Maoists to give up armed warfare and initiate dialogue, they described those like the ICI, which condemn the violence of both sides, as "apologists for the oppressors, in spite of their good intentions and sincere attitude."[111]

The Maoists claim to be fighting for socio-economic betterment of the tribals. But they are uneasy with NGOS that are working among the tribals. The Maoists resent the activists as they advocate a path different from their own to achieve socio-economic change. They are uneasy too with tribal organizations that pursue mass struggle to address grievances. They are known to undermine these struggles by infiltrating these organizations or their campaigns and provoking violence.

The intolerance of the State and the Maoists to peaceful, democratic ways of waging conflict is amply demonstrated by their attacks on non-

---

[109] Sudha Ramachandran, "India's War on Maoists under Attack," Asia Times Online, May 26, 2010, available online at http://www.atimes.com/atimes/South_Asia/LE26Df02.html, accessed on July 30, 2010.

[110] Praful Bidwai, " Dealing with Naxalism in Chhattisgarh," Transnational Institute, October 2007, available online at http://www.tni.org/article/dealing-naxalism-chhattisgarh , accessed on July 30, 2010.

[111] V Ganapathi, Letter to Independent Citizen Initiative dated Oct 10, 2006, available online at http://naxalrevolution.wordpress.com/2006/11/25/maoist-reply-to-independent-citizen-initiative-on-dantewada/, accessed on July 25, 2010

violent activists. Himanshu Kumar, a Gandhian, has been working in Dantewada among tribals for two decades. The Vanavasi Chetna Ashram, which he founded to provide legal aid to victims of violence, has experienced the wrath of the Salwa Judum, the security forces and Maoists. In 2009, the headquarters of his NGO in Kanwalnar in Dantewada was destroyed by CRPF and Chhattisgarh police personnel.

It is evident that the State and the Maoists are demolishing the democratic middle ground.

Maoist Governance

Besides waging armed conflict against the State and its functionaries as well as 'class enemies,' the Maoists have set up "parallel governments" in areas under their control. NGO activists say that in parts of rural Dandakaranya the civil administration has been absent for years, which makes the Maoist administration there not a "parallel administration" but the only one.[112] What is the nature of governance provided by the *janatana sarkar?* What kind of change have they brought in the lives of the tribals?

In many villages across the Dandakaranya region, government health centers and schools do not function as doctors and teachers rarely show up for work. Clinics and school buildings remain half-built with corrupt contractors unwilling to finish work they have been paid for. Forest officials demand bribes from tribals. By virtue of the gun they wield, the Maoists have been able to evoke fear in the local administration and among teachers, doctors and contractors, forcing them to work. They have forced *tendu* trade contractors to pay tribals higher wages for picking *tendu* leaves and cutting bamboo culms. Eminent civil liberties activist K. Balagopal pointed out that it is "the substantial increase they achieved in the payment for picking *tendu* leaf and the end they put to the oppressive domination of the headmen and *patwaris*" that contributed to the Maoists' "wide popularity...in the entire forest region abutting the Godaveri river in Telengana, Vidarbha and Chhattisgarh."[113] The Maoists have done much rural development work too.

---

[112] An NGO worker interviewed by the author at Khammam in Andhra Pradesh in June 2006.

[113] K. Balagopal, "Chhattisgarh: Physiognomy of Violence," Economic and Political Weekly 41, no. 22 (June 3-9, 2006): 2185.

They have helped tribals with construction of tanks, rainwater harvesting and land conservation works. Villagers testify that these works have improved their food security situation.[114]

However, questions have been raised about the Maoists' commitment to the well-being of the tribals. The government accuses Maoists of obstructing development in tribal areas and standing in the way of several initiatives that would improve the livelihood security of tribals. Besides they are said to be destroying the already limited infrastructure in Dandakaranya. Indeed Maoists have destroyed railway infrastructure, telecom towers and power stations.[115] They have blown up schools, health centers, panchayat buildings and roads, "thus destroying infrastructure needed for taking development to the rural hinterland inhabited by tribals."[116] They are accused of being anti-development.[117]

In their study on the impact of MGNREGA, researchers Kaustav Banerjee and Partha Saha point to a more complex picture. They argue that the MGNREGA is doing well in districts that are among the worst-hit by the Maoist conflict, such as Bastar, for instance. People are getting better wages in these districts because of Maoist pressure. Of all the permissible works under the MGNREGA, only road construction is being blocked by the Maoists as better roads will facilitate movement of security personnel. They are not obstructing other work such as afforestation, minor irrigation, land development, etc.[118]

---

[114] See not 39 above.

[115] P. V. Ramana, Maoists' Attack on Infrastructure, IDSA Comment, February 29, 2009, available online at http://www.idsa.in/idsastrategiccomments/MaoistsAttackson Infrastructure_PVRamana_200209, last accessed on July 25, 2010.

[116] Kanchan Gupta, "Two eyes for an eye, the jaw for a tooth,"The Pioneer, February 21, 2010, available online at http://www.dailypioneer.com/237428/Two-eyes-for-an-eye-the-jaw-for-a-tooth.html, accessed on July 30, 2010.

[117] "The Naxalites are anti-development and have targeted the very instruments of development - school buildings, roads, telephone towers etc. They know that development will wean the masses away, especially poor tribals, from the grip of Naxalites," Chidambaram said at a Chief Ministers' Conference on Internal Security. The Hindu, August 17, 2009, available online at http://www.thehindu.com/news/national/article4285.ece, accessed on July 30, 2010.

[118] Kaustav Banerjee and Partha Saha, "The NREGA, the Maoists and the Developmental Woes of the Indian State," EPW, 45, no. 28 (July 10, 2010).

Human rights activist Gautam Navlakha, who spent a fortnight with the Maoists in the Dandakaranya forests, says that the Maoists encourage education. The 'people's government' has prepared books that are being used to teach mathematics, social science, politics and Hindi, and books on the history of Dandakaranya, culture, biology and general science are under preparation. Books are written in the local Gondi language.[119] The Maoists consciously promote Gondi language and literature.[120] According to journalist Shubhranshu Choudhary, the books prepared by the Maoists emphasize the history of the tribal people with pictures of leaders like Birsa Munda. "There is also the predictable familiarization with icons like Mao and Marx and Indian leaders like Charu Mazumdar and Kanai Chatterjee," he says. Besides ideological indoctrination, the books provide practical information that could improve tribal lives, like tips on basic health and hygiene. The books carry pictures stressing the importance of washing hands before eating, boiling water before drinking it and sleeping under a mosquito net.[121] In a region where malaria, elephantiasis and cholera are rampant, Maoist education provides public health information too. Thus, the Maoists have stepped in to fill in the gap in public health and school facilities in tribal areas. They have acted not only to correct the government's failure to provide tribals with education and to foster tribal culture and language but also, they are using education to get multiple messages across to the people.

With regard to tribal traditions and customs that undermine women, the Maoists appear to be acting to tackle these but treading slowly. KAMS has campaigned against forced marriage and bigamy and the custom of making menstruating women live in a separate hut in the forests. Its achievements have been mixed. Changing mindsets has not been easy. For instance, the Maoists have been trying to change the practice of not allowing women to sow seeds. At public meetings men say they should be allowed to do so. Yet

---

[119] Gautam Navlakha, "Days and Nights in the Heartland of Rebellion,"Economic and Political Weekly, 45, no. 16 (April 17- 23, 2010).

[120] People's March, 7, no. 1, January 2006, 7, cited in Sundar, "Bastar, Maoists and Salwa Judum," 3190.

[121] Debarshi Dasgupta, "My Book is Red,"Outlook,May 17, 2010, available online at http://www.outlookindia.com/article.aspx?265325, accessed on July 1, 2010.

they are unwilling to permit this in practice. So the Maoists allow women to sow seeds on common land belonging to the janatana sarkar.[122] They seem reluctant to force social change that could cost them public support and hence, prefer to move slowly on these matters.

Navlakha notes the "prominent role of women in the movement" and the sharing of all work by both sexes. Women constitute 40 percent of those in administrative jobs, and the Maoists aim to make this 50 percent, he says.[123] While there are a significant number of women Maoists in the political as well as military wings of the Maoist movement, their role in the top decision making bodies is still marginal. Only one woman – Anuradha Ghandy – has been part of the politburo so far. Vasanth Kannabiran draws attention to the "stereotypical and hierarchical masculinities and femininities that inform the [Maoist] movement even at the highest levels."[124]

A worrying feature of Maoist governance is their justice system. It is swift but crude and brutal raising the question whether it can be treated as justice at all. 'Class enemies' are executed as are tribals who are critical of their actions or who are suspected to be informers. *Jan adalats* are held to punish offenders. In the words of Subba Atish, a former Maoist:

> *The jan adalat is organized by the commander or deputy commander of a dalam [armed squad]. They get about 15 villages together and pass a sentence. Members of the area committee, range committee head, and divisional committee will pass the sentence. They [accused] are usually supposed to be given a chance to defend themselves but generally this is how it works - first they are brought and beaten, and by the time the beating is over they are so scared that they will admit to the crime. Villagers and relatives who come to their defense are threatened and they*

---

[122] Arundhati Roy, "Walking with the Comrades,"Outlook,March 29, 2010, available online at http://www.outlookindia.com/article.aspx?264738-0, accessed on July 30, 2010.

[123] See note 119 above.

[124] Vasanth Kannabiran, Scattered truth, bitter seeds,"Seminar, 607, March 2010, available online at http://www.india-seminar.com/2010/607/607_vasanth_kannabiran.htm, accessed on July 30, 2010

don't have much of a defense in these adalats. If a relative says
something, the commander will say: "So you also are with him
[accused]? You want the same thing to happen to you?" ... [I]f
they [leaders] have made up their mind in the matter they tend
to ignore villagers' opinion. They will say, "This is an enemy. If
you want him punished, raise your hand." Even if the people say
"don't kill," if they [leaders] have decided to kill, they will. And
if they decide not to kill, even if the public says, "Kill, Kill," they
will not kill.[125]

Subba Atish goes on to describe how four people were executed in two *jan adalats* that he witnessed. Of the four, two were found guilty of conspiring against Maoist commanders and the other two of providing the police with information about a Maoist ambush. There was no opportunity for the 'guilty' to appeal the punishments, which were meted out soon after the verdict was pronounced. Describing the executions, he says, that the Maoists "tie a rope around each person's neck and two people stand on either side and pull the rope-ends till the person dies. All four were killed in the same manner."[126]

The Maoists commitment to prevent tribal exploitation is open to question. It is true that it was their efforts that successfully raised the wages of *tendu* leaf pickers in Andhra and Chhattisgarh. It is true too that they have backed tribals in their opposition to mining activity on their land. Yet, the Maoists have also acted to protect the exploiting classes. In 2005, for instance, they enforced a strike in *tendu* collection to thwart the government's attempt to do away with contractors and start co-operatives. Surely the proposed co-operatives would have contributed to reducing exploitation of tribals. Why then did they oppose the setting up of co-operatives? It is well known that Maoist 'taxes' on the *tendu* trade amounts to millions of rupees annually and is an important source of funding their activities. It is believed that the Maoists opposed co-operatives in the *tendu*

---

[125] Human Rights Watch *Being Neutral is our Biggest Crime: Government Vigilante, and Naxalite Abuses in India's Chhattisgarh State,* (New York: HRW, 2008), 98-99.

[126] Ibid., 99.

trade as this would cut out the contractors – their 'tax payers' - and eat into their sizeable revenue. Doing away with 'exploitative contractors', therefore, is not on the Maoist agenda. There is a similar relationship with mining companies. The latter are reported to be paying the Maoists massive sums as 'protection money'. The Maoists might denounce mining activity as 'loot of Adivasi resources' but it is unlikely they would want the mining companies to shut down operations and leave Dandakaranya. After all, mining companies are paying them millions of rupees, which fund their military operations.

Impact on India's Economic Growth

What impact is the extortion by Maoists and the violence in Dandakaranya having on investment and the economic climate? A 2009 report by the Federation of Indian Chambers of Commerce and Industry (FICCI) warns that the Maoist insurgency could "soon hurt some industrial investment plans." It laments that at a time "when India needs to ramp up its industrial machine to lock in growth and just when foreign companies are joining the party, the Naxalites are clashing with the mining and steel companies essential for India's long-term success."[127] Extraction of iron ore, coal, bauxite and other minerals are regarded as important for India to maintain its 8 percent economic growth rate.[128]

Tribal protests and Maoist violence seem to be coming in the way of these plans. For instance, mass protests compelled the Tata Group to alter production plans for its small car project. It was forced to move out of Singur in West Bengal. Vedanta's plans in Niyamgiri have run aground. Several mining projects such as Arcelor Mittal's $9 billion steel projects in Jharkhand and Orissa, the South Korean steel giant Pohang Iron and Steel

---

[127] Ashish Kothari, "Behind the concern,"Frontline, 7, no. 4, Feb 13-26, 2010, available online at http://www.frontlineonnet.com/fl2704/stories/20100226270408800.htm, last accessed on July 22, 2010.

[128] As finance minister, Chidambaram told an audience at Harvard University that India "should mine these resources quickly and efficiently." See his speech at the Harvard University's South Asia Initiative, The Harish C. Mahindra 2007 Lecture on "Poor Rich Countries: The Challenges of Development," available online at http://www.indianembassy.org/page. php?id=697, accessed on July 22, 2010.

Company (POSCO)'s $ 32 billion steel project at Jagatsinghpur in Orissa and Jindal Steel Works' $7 billion steel plant at Salboni in West Bengal have been stalled due to Maoist violence in these states. Maoist attacks have affected production too. Bauxite production at NALCO, for instance, has fallen by 20 percent since a Maoist attack on their mines in April 2009. Attacks on mining companies have hit exports. Coal Minister Shriprakash Jaiswal has claimed that coal production has the potential to increase by 25 percent if Maoist violence stopped. The Maoists have damaged telecom and power infrastructure. They have repeatedly targeted railway infrastructure, including freight trains. *Bandhs* imposed by them have paralyzed economic activity and resulted in loss of business running into crores of rupees.[129]

Focus on Development

The multiple costs inflicted by the conflict, especially the impact on India's economic growth, has pushed the government to take the Maoist problem seriously. Under criticism for its excessively militaristic approach and realizing the importance of addressing tribal grievances for successful tackling of the Maoist problem, the government has begun giving attention to the socio-economic development of areas worst hit by the violence. It is considering an Integrated Action Plan (IAP) for 60 districts worst affected by the conflict. The plan is being implemented not only in those districts that are in the armed conflict zone but also those where Maoist activity is "incipient". Before implementation of the IAP begins, steps will be taken to improve governance in these districts to ensure that the massive funds being pumped here do reach the intended beneficiaries. This will include measure to ensure full implementation of PESA and FRA, as well as schemes like the PDS and the MGNREGA. [130] It is evident that the government has finally woken up to the fact that enacting legislation, drawing up elaborate poverty-fighting schemes and allocating funds is not enough. These have

---

[129] Ajit Kumar Singh, "Maoists: Targeting the Economy," South Asia Intelligence Review (SAIR), 8, no. 51, June 28, 2010, available online at http://www.satp.org/satporgtp/sair/Archives/sair8/8_51.htm, accessed on July 14, 2010.

[130] The Hindu, August 8, 2010, available online at http://www.hindu.com/2010/08/08/stories/2010080855971300.htm, last accessed on September 19, 2010.

to be implemented in letter and spirit to ensure that the benefits reach the poorest and most marginalized sections in this country. The first steps in this direction seem to have been taken.

The costs of the Maoist conflict have also forced the government to review its mining policy. A new legislation under consideration seeks to make tribals stakeholders in mining activities. The draft Mines and Minerals (Development and Regulation) Bill 2010 provides for 26 percent partnership in the company to people living in an area over which a mining lease is granted. While this is a step in the right direction, whether the powerful mining lobby will allow it to be enacted remains to be seen.[131]

The Way Forward

The Maoist conflict in Dandakaranya has drawn attention to the immense injustices suffered by the rural poor. It has forced the government to begin addressing the tribal grievances underlying it. Several legislations that provide for greater tribal autonomy or address the problem of tribal land dispossession have been enacted in response to the conflict. Socio-economic programs too have been put in place to reduce the crushing impact of poverty. The Maoists too have sought to bring positive socio-economic change in the areas they control.

However, the predominantly violent waging of conflict by the two main adversaries is wiping out whatever positive impact the State or the Maoists have done to address poverty. It has unleashed human suffering on a far greater scale than existed before. It is accentuating poverty and triggering new conflicts and grievances. The Maoists use of arms to secure justice for the tribals is resulting in new injustices. It is attracting more violence by the State. As for the State, its use of force to quell the conflict is worsening it. It has taken the violence to a new, higher level. Its adoption of economic policies and development paradigms that bring benefits to a few at the cost of others is worsening the distress underlying the conflict. The evolution of

---

[131] Sudha Ramachandran, "India digs deep to outflank Maoists," Asia Times Online, August, 4, 2010, available online at http://www.atimes.com/atimes/South_Asia/LH04Df04.html, accessed on September 18, 2010.

the conflict over the past several decades shows that the use of force has not worked for any of the main parties. It has not brought the Maoists closer to their goal. Rather thousands of their cadres, leaders and sympathizers have been consumed by the violence. The State has been able to put a lid on the violence from time to time but the conflict has re-emerged with renewed fury in a few years.

The use of force by the State and the Maoists is deepening the intractability of the conflict. It has drawn more parties and vested interests into the conflict over the decades. The complexity of the conflict has grown with violence generating more problems. If six decades ago, the conflict was one primarily over poverty generated by feudal exploitation, today there are issues such as corporate greed, rampant vigilantism, proliferation of weapons and militarization of society that have added to the conflict's complexity. It is obvious from the conflict's evolution over the decades that the spiral of violence that has engulfed vast stretches of the country cannot be broken with more violence.

It is only through halting violence and engaging in dialogue that the spiral of violence can begin to be broken. The root causes need to be addressed. It requires land reform. Mere legislation will not resolve problems. These need to be implemented in letter and spirit. Similarly, socio-economic programs must be implemented in a way that benefits reach the poorest sections of our society.

While big business is concerned about tribal protests and the Maoist violence, it is not overly concerned about the escalating violence on account of the government's military strategy. It is widely believed in business circles that Operation Green Hunt will ultimately eliminate the tribals and the Maoists, and free the mineral rich land for them to exploit. While Operation Green Hunt and other military strategies might quell the violence it will not resolve the problem. Tribal unrest will persist so long as the underlying issues are not resolved.

STATE RESPONSE TO THE MAOIST CHALLENGE: AN OVERVIEW

P V Ramana

Naxalites of the Communist Party of India (Maoist), or CPI (Maoist), in short, have been waging an armed struggle, which they term as protracted people's war (PPW), for the capture/seizure of state/political power in India since 1967. Following a series of mergers and splits in the Naxalite movement, the two largest of these outfits, Communist Party of India — Marxist-Leninist (People's War), or CPI-ML (PW), popularly known as the PWG, and the Maoist Communist Centre of India (MCCI), popularly known as MCC, merged on September 21, 2004 to found the CPI (Maoist).

Presently, according to the Union Home Minister, 223 districts in 20 States are variously affected by the Maoist challenge — moderate to intense[1]. All along, seizure of political power or state power has remained the consistent and ultimate objective of the rebels. As one author correctly observed, "The real aim of the Naxalites is neither the domain of economics nor state welfare. It is a political movement having its goal as the seizure of political power i.e. state power…[2]" The objective of this paper is to present an overview of the responses of the Union government and briefly that of the affected States to the Maoist challenge.

---

[1] Speech of the Hon'ble Home Minister Shri P. Chidambaram on the occasion of DGPs / IGPs Conference 2009, New Delhi, September 14, 2009 http://www.mha.nic.in/pdfs/HM-DGP-CONF140909.pdf, (accessed on 31 January 2011)

[2] S Subramanian, "Naxalism: Fact, Fiction and Future", Paper presented at the "Workshop on Naxalism: A Distortion of Democratic Development", Rajaji International Institute for Public Affairs and Public Administration (RIIPAA), Hyderabad, April 7, 1990. S. Subramanian was the then Director of SVP National Police Academy (NPA).

Union Government Response

The Maoist challenge attracted the serious attention of the Union government for the first time in 1998, when a Coordination Centre was constituted in the Ministry of Home Affairs (MHA) headed by the Home Secretary, following heightened violence by the rebels in 1997. The members of the Coordination Centre included the Directors Generals of Police (DGP) of Maharashta, Madhya Pradesh, Andhra Pradesh and Orissa. Overtime, the membership of the Coordination Centre has been enlarged to include DGP of some more states as the spatial spread of the Maoists, their influence and violence spread, to, now, include 16 States.

The MHA, in 1998, suggested to the affected States to formulate a 'holistic' security and development plan to deal with the issue comprehensively. While the affected States procrastinated in formulating and submitting their action plans, the MHA, too, took a rather lighter view of the challenge.

On the other hand, the Maoists were operating according to a plan in a determined fashion and methodically. In 2001, the then PWG conducted its Third Congress and decided to declare some areas as guerrilla zones, which resulted in increased violence by the rebels;[3]. At the same time, since then, the Maoists also began to penetrate virgin territories. Besides, their lethal arsenal began to acquire greater sophistication after they began to seize weapons from the Security Forces (SFs) in attacks on police stations, armouries and in ambushes and raids on patrol parties.

While these two important trends (increasing militarization and spatial expansion) continued ever since 2001, the CPI (Maoist) was founded and it held its first Unity Ninth Congress in January 2007. Following the Unity

---

[3] There are three stages in the revolutionary movement viz. 'organisational phase' in which the focus is on conducting struggles on people's issues and violence is selective, even as they are on a defensive mode vis-à-vis the state; 'guerrilla phase' in which the rebels perceive themselves to be on equal footing vis-à-vis the state, and violence reaches a crescendo; 'mobile warfare phase' in which the rebels enjoy an upper hand vis-à-vis the state and are on a 'strategic offensive'. Presently, the rebels are in the mobile warfare phase in the Dandakaranya region of Chhattisgarh. The explanation offered here is derived form K Srinivas Reddy, "The Maoist Challenge", Seminar, No. 569, (January 2007)

Congress, the violence and actions committed by the Maoists touched alarmingly new heights.

On the other hand, the Union government denied the extent of the Maoist challenge for a number of years and its officers gave out contradictory information on the spatial spread of the Maoists for many years, before eventually admitting the extent of the spatial spread, as the Union Home Minister did in 2009, as mentioned above.

All along, the Union government held the view that the response would be two-fold, development and security. The same has been repeatedly emphasised by the incumbent government[4]. Nevertheless, the emphasis has been more on militarily dealing with the Maoists.

Divergent Perceptions of Magnitude

It is remarkably striking that, for a number of years, the various high-level officers of the Central government had widely divergent perceptions of the extent of the spread of the Maoists. Thus, speaking in the Lok Sabha on May 22, 2006, the Home Minister said: "I have personally collected data... only 50 districts are affected". But, the Prime Minister had some other statistics to offer. He said, during a meeting of Standing Committee of Chief Ministers of Naxalite affected States, on April 13, 2006, that the Naxalite movement "has now spread to over-160 districts".

This lack of coherence continued into the next year. Replying to an unstarred question number 320 in the Rajya Sabha, on November 21, 2007, the Minister of State (MoS) for Home Affairs said 91 districts in 11 States were affected by Maoist violence. On the other hand, the then Cabinet Secretary, BK Chaturvedi, while speaking at the annual Conference of Chief Secretaries, in New Delhi, said, seven months earlier, on April 20, 2007 that a total of 182 districts in 16 States were Maoist affected.

But, Mallojula Venugopal alias Sonu alias Bhupathi, who is in-charge of the Dandakaranya Special Zone Committee (DKSZC) in the Central

---

[4] For instance, see " PM's Speech at the Chief Minister's Conference on Internal Security" December 20, 2007, New Delhi, http://pmindia.nic.in/speech/content.asp?id=632 (accessed on 31 January 2011)

Committee of the rebels, told *People's March*, a Maoist mouthpiece, in July 2007: "… our party has a presence in 17 States…"

Further, a former Governor of Chhattisgarh perceives that the rebels have a far greater presence. He said in an interview to a website in 2007, "I would like to share that currently from the figures I have been able to obtain, 256 districts have been declared as [N]axalite affected districts…"

Incomprehensibly so, without affording any reason the MHA suddenly changed the parameters of determining the affected areas. Thus, for the first time, in its Annual Report 2005-2006, the MHA gave statistics of number of police stations from which violent activities of the Maoists were reported, but maintained silence on the number of police stations in which the rebels have a presence and influence. Ever since, it has maintained this parameter.

In 2008, a 'newer' parameter was introduced: number of villages from which rebel violence was reported, and this as a percentage of the total number of villages in the country. Thus, the Rajya Sabha was informed on March 19, 2008 that a 'mere 14,000 villages out of a total of 650,000 villages are Maoist affected, which accounts for just two per cent of the total number of villages in the country'. Moreover, the Rajya Sabha was also informed that 'the number of Naxal violence related incidents at 700 accounts for a mere 1.1 per cent of the total extremist related incidents in the country'.

From the foregoing, one is persuaded to argue that these efforts were meant to 'manage people's perception' of the intensity of the problem, rather than vigorously pursue the MHA's "Public Perception Management"[5] efforts — which is an element of the triad of the Centre's response to the Maoist challenge. Eventually in 2009, the Union Home Minister admitted that the Maoists have a presence in 223 districts across 29 States.

---

[5] Within the context of addressing the Naxalite issue, the MHA seems to be of the view that it would constitute issuing advertisements in newspapers at frequent intervals, approximately one every month, and hosting tribal youth exchange programmes involving hundreds of tribal youth in affected areas. For instance, see Ministry of Home Affairs, "Action Plan – III, October 2009 to March 2010", New Delhi: Ministry of Home Affairs, available online at http://www.mha.nic.in/pdfs/AAP-III.pdf.

14-Point Policy to Deal with the Maoist Challenge

The Union government, in March 2006, spelt out its 14-point policy to deal with the Maoist challenge[6]. These are as follows:

(i) The Government will deal sternly with the naxalites indulging in violence.

(ii) Keeping in view that naxalism is not merely a law & order problem, the policy of the Govt. is to address this menace simultaneously on political security, development and public perception management fronts in a holistic manner.

(iii) Naxalism being an inter–state problem, the states will adopt a collective approach and pursue a coordinated response to counter it.

(iv) The states will need to further improve police response and pursue effective and sustained police action against naxalites and their infrastructure individually and jointly.

(v) There will be no peace dialogue by the affected states with the naxal groups unless the latter agrees to give up violence and arms.

(vi) Political parties must strengthen their cadre base in naxal affected areas so that the potential youth there can be weaned away from the path of naxal ideology.

(vii) The states from where naxal activity/influence, and not naxal violence, is reported should have a different approach with special focus on accelerated socio-economic development of the backward areas and regular inter action with NGOs, intelligentsia, civil liberties groups etc. to minimize over ground support for the naxalite ideology and activity.

(viii) Efforts will continue to be made to promote local resistance groups against naxalites but in a manner that the villagers are provided

---

[6] See Status Paper on the Naxal Problem, Internal Security Division, Ministry of Home Affairs, New Delhi, March 13, 2006.

adequate security cover and the area is effectively dominated by the security forces.

(ix) Mass media should also be extensively used to highlight the futility of naxal violence and loss of life and property caused by it and developmental schemes of the Government in the affected areas so as to restore people's faith and confidence in the Government machinery.

(x) The states should announce a suitable transfer policy for the naxal affected districts. Willing, committed and competent officers will need to be posted with a stable tenure in the naxal affected districts. These officers will also need to be given greater delegation and flexibility to deliver better and step up Government presence in these areas.

(xi) The Government of Andhra Pradesh has an effective surrender and rehabilitation policy for naxalites and has produced good results over the years. The other states should adopt a similar policy.

(xii) The State Governments will need to accord a higher priority in their annual plans to ensure faster socio- economic development of the naxal affected areas. The focus areas should be to distribute land to the landless poor as part of the speedy implementation of the land reforms, ensure development of physical infrastructure like roads, communication, power etc. and provide employment opportunities to the youth in these areas.

(xiii) Another related issue is that development activities are not undertaken in some of the naxalite affected areas mainly due to extortion, threat or fear from the naxalite cadres. In these areas, even contractors are not coming forward to take up developmental work. Adequate security and other measures would need to be taken to facilitate uninterrupted developmental activities in the naxal affected areas.

(xiv) The Central Government will continue to supplement the efforts and resources of the affected states on both security and development fronts and bring greater coordination between the states to successfully tackle the problem.

Development Responses

Past and Present Schemes

The Union government has initiated a number of development programmes and schemes, some of them especially targeting the Maoist affected districts. The objective of these programmes and schemes is to bring in rapid socio-economic development and fill critical gaps in infrastructure. These various programmes include:

- Pradhan Mantri Grameen Sadak Yojana (PMGSY).[7]

- National Rural Employment Guarantee Programme (NREGP).[8]

- The earlier Backward Districts Initiative[9] — a component of Rashtriya Sam Vikas Yojana (RSVY) — now subsumed into the Backward Regions Grant Fund (BRGF).[10]

- Indira Aawas Yojana.

- Grameen Vidyuti Karan Yojana.

---

[7] The programme is aimed at building rural roads to improve connectivity. "The State Governments have been requested to identify and prioritize unconnected habitations having population of 500 and above in plain areas and 250 and above in tribal areas for preparing detailed project reports as per PMGSY programme guidelines". See Annual Report, 2007-2008, Ministry of Home Affairs, Government of India, p. 22; also see the official website of PMGSY, http://www.pmgsy.nic.in/

[8] It was originally initiated in 200 districts, and was extended to 330 districts in April 2007. Presently, it is being implemented in all the districts of the country.

[9] BDI scheme was launched during the financial year 2003-2004, "with the main objective of putting in place programmes and policies with the joint efforts of the Centre and States which would remove barriers of growth, accelerate the development process and improve the quality of life of the people. The scheme aims at focussed development of backward areas which would help reduce imbalances and speed up development ". See Planning Commission, MLP Division, "Backward Districts Initiative – Rashtriya Sam Vikas Yojana – The Scheme and Guidelines for Preparation of District Plans", p.1, http://www.planningcommission.nic.in/plans/stateplan/guid_rsvy.pdf. (accessed on 7 May, 2008). Also, BDI was intended to "address the problems of low agricultural productivity, unemployment and to fill critical gaps in physical and social infrastructure".

[10] The BDI was implemented in 147 districts, whereas the BRGF is being implemented in 250 districts.

- Bharat Nirman.

- National Rural Health Mission.

- Sarva Siksha Abhiyan.

- Integrated Child Development Services (ICDS).

"These schemes are in addition to various income-generating, public-utility and social-security schemes of different Ministries like Rural Development, Agriculture, Health and Family Welfare, Youth Affairs and Sports, Panchayati Raj and Tribal Affairs[11]". When the RSVY, and its integral component BDI, were replaced with BRGF, in August 2006, it was decided that each district would first complete drawing the Rs 45 cr it is entitled to under the BDI before it is allowed to shift to drawing funds under BRGF.

Pilot Project

In October 2007, the Union government announced that rapid socio-economic development would be brought-in in a comprehensive manner in eight districts in four States as a Pilot Project[12]. Subsequently, the Prime Minister, in his December 20, 2007 address to the Conference of Chief Ministers on Internal Security, noted that this programme was being extended to 33 districts in eight States[13].

---

[11] The Minister of State for Home Affairs informed the Lok Sabha in reply to a Starred Question on April 22, 2008, "Press Release: Development Initiatives in Naxalite-affected Districts", April 22, 2008, http://pib.nic.in/release/release.asp?relid=37724&kwd=, (accessed on 7 May, 2008)

[12] These districts include Aurangabad and Gaya in Bihar; Bijapur and Dantewada in Chhattisgarh; Chhatra, and Palamu in Jharkhand; and Malkangiri and Raygada in Orissa.

[13] These include 10 in Jharkhand, seven in Chhattisgarh, six in Bihar, five in Orissa, two in Maharashtra and one each in Andhra Pradesh, Madhya Pradesh and Uttar Pradesh. The Inter Ministerial Group that monitors this project has met seven times until now. The last meeting, held on April 16, 2008, reviewed the progress of development schemes in the 33 districts, and had, reportedly, "clearly determined the course of action in respect of development measures envisaged in the integrated security and development action plans", http://www.thaindian.com/newsportal/south-asia/7th-inter-ministerial-grouping-meeting-, (accessed on 17 April 2008)

Task Force

Besides, Task Force under the chairmanship of the Cabinet Secretary was constituted on February 12, 2008 "to promote coordinated efforts across a range of development and security activities so that problems in the naxal affected areas can be tackled in a comprehensive manner.[14]"

Unified Action Plan

Following the constitution of the Task Force mentioned above, on November 24, 2010 the Union Cabinet approved a proposal to launch a programme known as Unified Action Plan (UAP), which was originally known as Integrated Action Plan, at an estimated budget of Rs 13,742 cr to herald rapid socio-economic development in Naxalite affected districts. Initially, the programme would be implemented in 35 districts and gradually expanded to cover 60 districts. This Planning Commission designed programme shall be implemented at the district-level by a committee comprising the District Collector, Superintendent of Police and District Forest Officer. At the state-level it would be monitored by the Development Commissioner and by the Planning Commission at the national level. The Union Cabinet disagreed with the implementation mechanism suggested by the Planning Commission and suggested the above mechanism for implementation and monitoring.[15]

Assessment: Tardy Implementation, Weak monitoring, Leakages

Implementation and Monitoring: As Parliament was informed in April 2008, nearly five years after the RSVY scheme was launched, of the total Rs 6615 crore earmarked, at the time it was "subsumed into the Backward Regions Grant Fund (BRGF) Programme in August 2006, the districts concerned had claimed only Rs 2850 crore[16]." In other words, the districts concerned

---

[14] Ministry of Home Affairs, Annual Report, 2007-2008, p. 20.

[15] See http://www.hindustantimes.com/Cabinet-plan-for-Naxal-areas-retrogressive/ Article1-649227.aspx#. Accessed on 17 January 2011.

[16] See the reply by Minister for Panchayati Raj to Lok Sabha Unstarred Question No.2240, "Review of Rashtriya Sam Vikas Yojana", answered on April 23, 2008, New Delhi, Rajya Sabha Secretariat. The Minister further informed that of the 147 districts under the RSVY, as on that date, a mere 70 districts claimed their full entitlement of Rs 45 cr; 39 districts had to claim the last installment; 30 districts two more installments; and eight districts had to claim three or more installments.

could utilise a mere 43% of the allocated funds.

The implementation of these development schemes has been rather tardy, and its monitoring was weak. In its 126th Report tabled in the Lok Sabha on April 26, 2007, the Parliamentary Standing Committee on Home Affairs noted:

"The Committee however, feels that there is no perceptible change on the socio-economic front. Though the socio-economic development cannot be quantified, it can be perceived and if such a perceptible change is there, undoubtedly it will have a lasting impact. The Committee ... recommends that various schemes under the Ministries of Rural Development and other Ministries may also be implemented for the socio-economic development in the naxal affected areas. There needs to be an effective monitoring mechanism on the implementation of these schemes with the involvement of all the concerned Ministries and agencies."

The reasons for deficient delivery are not far to seek. What a Steering Group of the Planning Commission noted in 2001 is equally true today, too. It said[17]:

"The Working Groups strongly felt that though the programmes for poverty alleviation were well designed, poor delivery was a major hurdle in eradicating poverty. It was felt that the Government machinery at the cutting edge level was too thinly spread, poorly trained and ill equipped to implement programmes, which require not only commitment to poor but also certain amount of technical expertise. The groups felt that given the outreach of the Government, the administrative machinery has to be strengthened by reforming it from within, by providing support through networking with other institutions and by subjecting it to greater supervision and control by the Panchayati Raj institutions (PRIs) and other Community

---

[17] Planning Commission of India, Report of the Steering Group on Rural Poverty Alleviation, Watershed Development, Decentralised Planning and Panchayati Raj Institutions, for the Tenth Five Year Plan, 2002-2007, TYFP SC Report No.8/2001, November 2001, New Delhi, p. 36. The Members of the Group included Secretary, Union Ministry of Rural Development, Rural Development Secretaries of various States, well-known economists such as Prof Hanuamntha Rao, Prof Indira Hiraway, Prof Gopal Chadha, and Ms Renana Jhabwala of SEWA, etc.

Based Organisations (CBOs)."

Leakages: Besides, siphoning-off funds/leakages is a significant contributing factor in the benefits not reaching the targeted groups[18]. The situation, indeed, reminds one of what former Prime Minister Rajiv Gandhi said. During a visit to Kalahandi, Orissa, in 1985, he said: "Of every rupee spent by the government, only 17 paise reached the intended beneficiary"[19]. Speaking from Bundelkhand, Uttar Pradesh, about the implementation of, and rampant misappropriation in, the NREGS, Member of Parliament Rahul Gandhi reportedly said, "Now the situation is even worse"[20]. He went to add that he had seen job cards of 50 people "with the same serial number, and not even one card had the entry of work"[21].

Pilot Project

The question is: would some other districts be selected if they report similar levels of violence? or would any of the 33 districts be taken-off the list if they did not report the same level of violence in the succeeding years? Moreover, as anyone familiar with the Maoist scheme of things would know, the degree of violence can never be a true indicator of the presence and influence of the rebels in any area. If the Maoists decide to stage a 'tactical retreat', then there would be no violence committed by them. Besides, if the rebels enjoy unquestioned hold and sway over an area, and the State is not conducting any anti-Maoist operations, then too, no violence would be reported. It could

---

[18] Personal communication from a Superintendent of Police (SP) of a district in the south Telengana region of Andhra Pradesh, March 2008. Under the NREGS about Rs 200 cr has been allotted to each district. In this particular district not much money has been spent, on the ground that wheeler-dealers would siphon-off funds. Thus, a huge amount has been left unspent. The approximate amount of misappropriation is over 50 lakh per mandal (taluq); and there are 66 mandals in that district. Besides, there is total mayhem in the villages at the meetings of social audit parties, with the wheeler-dealers (local Legislator's henchmen) creating disorder. There have also been instances when members of the social audit parties were threatened and manhandled.

[19] Santosh K Joy, "Rahul echoes Rajiv Gandhi's comments on public funds", Rediff News, http://www.rediff.com/news/2008/jan/17rahul.htm, January 17, 2008 (accessed on 31 January 2011)

[20] Ibid.

[21] Ibid.

be debated if the criterion could have been sustained presence and influence in the highest number of villages/ hamlets, in each district.

This new initiative has just been launched and it is too early to make any assessment of its efficacy/usefulness.

Security Response

As has been noted by a number of analysts, the response of the Centre, and the governments in the various affected States, has largely been military oriented, or crushing the Maoists militarily through security force operations; in some States, in fact, both the security response and the development response are weak.

Assistance and Guidelines

The Centre has been assisting the States in a number of ways in militarily dealing with the rebels. It has advised the states to strengthen intelligence gathering mechanism, augment police force, fortify police stations, provide incentives, impart specialised training to the police in jungle warfare, etc. On its part, the Centre has been sending Central Para Military Forces upon request by the States, extending financial assistance for the Modernisation of Police Forces (MPF) and providing 100 per cent financial assistance under the Security Related Expenditure (SRE) scheme for various expenses incurred by the affected States[22].

Assessment of SRE and MPF allocation-utilisation

The last of these, *i.e.* SRE, is discussed in this passage to describe some of the dilemmas and consequent responses for better utilisation of amounts that have been earmarked. The SRE scheme is implemented on a re-imbursement basis. The MHA informed the Parliamentary Standing Committee on Home Affairs that, until 2005, that:

    (a) Only 50% of the expenditure was reimbursed,

---

[22] For details of SRE Guidelines, see Annex I.

(b) States were always under financial constraints, and were, thus, hesitant to commit funds[23].

Thus, the MHA has decided to implement 100% reimbursement, and had also revised the guidelines for including districts under the SRE. In fact, during 2004-2005, of the total Rs 29,20,000 crore budgeted for SRE — to insurgency hit states of Jammu and Kashmir, the North East and Naxalite-affected States — 14,97,529 crore was utilised by the States, and the balance 14,22,471 crore was "saved". In view of the fact that the guidelines have been revised, and reimbursement has been made 100%, the Committee hoped that there would be better utilisation of funds. As the following table indicates, those hopes have only been partially met.

Table 1: SRE Reimbursement to Naxalite-affected States, 2006-2009

S. No	States	2006-2007	2007-2008	2008-2009
1	Andhra Pradesh	6.1	5.0	308.79
2	Bihar	0.04	2.30	305.18
3	Chhattisgarh	9.68	6.50	1540.69
4	Jharkhand	14.72	4.40	1876.25
5	Madhya Pradesh	2.51	1.70	381.36
6	Maharashtra	5.26	3.70	389.49
7	Orissa	7.16	6.73	969.91
8	Uttar Pradesh	Ñ	0.80	111.46
9	West Bengal	1.50	2.80	100.19

Source: Adapted from the Annexure to the Reply to Lok Sabha Starred Question No. 276, answered on December 4, 2007, New Delhi: Lok Sabha Secretariat; and http://mha.nic.in/pdfs/NM-Annex-IV.pdf.

Note: Data in crores of rupees.

---

[23] Government of India, Parliamentary Standing Committee on Home Affairs, 112th Report, Demands for Grants, 2005-2006, New Delhi: Rajya Sabha Secretariat, April 2005.

In the case of MPF allocations, too, the utilisation has not been full. Thus, for instance, of the Rs 1190.63 crore (Budget Estimates – BE) for 2007-2008, as on March 7, 2008 only Rs 834.96 crore have been utilised by the States, thus rendering unutilised Rs 355.67 crore [24]. In this wake, the Parliamentary Standing Committee on Home Affairs, during the hearings on Demands for Grants observed, thus, about the implementation and monitoring of the MPF scheme[25]:

> ... the role of the Ministry is not confined to merely allocating funds to the States but it has the responsibility to ensure that each and every rupee is spent in the furtherance of the objective of the scheme. The Committee reiterates its recommendations made in the earlier reports that it should be insisted upon all the States to send utilization certificates at the earliest in order to ensure that States spend the funds meant for modernization of their police forces in an efficient manner.

Security-Centric Centre

In 2005, the Home Ministry had constituted a committee comprising Director Generals of some of the affected States, Director General of Central Police Reserve Force (CRPF) and top officials of the Intelligence Bureau (IB). In its report, the Committee noted[26]:

> While the mechanism constituted for countering naxalism envisaged a multi-pronged approach, over the years the State response has tended to remain largely police centric, with the main effort being to counter the movement with superior force. The approach has often swung from one extreme – that of using overwhelming force-to the other, structured around 'ceasefires' and

---

[24] Government of India, Parliamentary Standing Committee on Home Affairs, 132nd Report, "Demands for Grants, 2008-2009", New Delhi: Rajya Sabha Secretariat, April 2008; and Annexure Referred to in paras (a) and (b) of Rajya Sabha Unstarred Question No. 1312, answered on March 12, 2008, New Delhi, Rajya Sabha Secretariat.

[25] Government of India, Parliamentary Standing Committee on Home Affairs, 132nd Report, "Demands for Grants, 2008-2009", New Delhi: Rajya Sabha Secretariat, April 2008.

[26] Cited from an internal report of the Ministry of Home Affairs. Copy available with the author.

'peace talks'. While it is recognized that the naxal problem goes well beyond mere law and order dimensions, the broader socio-economic issues have not attracted serious attention...

Even now, there does not seem to be a radical change in the government's orientation, not withstanding the fact that 33 districts have been selected for rapid socio-economic development. In his December 20, 2007 speech the Prime Minister said: "... affected states must set up Special Task Forces on the Andhra Pradesh pattern and the Centre will provide assistance for this purpose. I would also urge the Home Ministry to also consider establishing a dedicated trained force at the Centre either as part of an existing force or as a separate one"[27]. In fact, an expert panel constituted by the Planning Commission, which had submitted its report in late-April 2008, is also of the view that state response has largely been military–oriented[28]. Its Member Secretary was reported to have said, quoting from the Panel's Report, that the Centre's response has been "heavily security-centric." For instance, at the first meeting of the Empowered Group of Ministers (EGoM) that was constituted to comprehensively address the Naxalite-issue, the focus was essentially on 'security response', while 'development response' was near totally ignored. According to a media report of February 19, 2007: "... the EGoM ... focussed on strengthening intelligence gathering and better coordination among affected States... it was also decided to provide better training to police personnel and furnish the States with latest equipment to deal with the menace..."

CAIT Schools : The MHA issued directives to start 20 Counter Insurgency and Anti-Terrorist (CIAT) Schools, to impart specialised training to State police personnel counter insurgency operations, jungle warfare and terrorism in some of the affected States such as Bihar, Chhattisgarh, Orissa and Jharkhand. Of these, seven CIAT schools in four affected States of Bihar (1), Chhattisgarh (2), Jharkhand (2) and Orissa (2), have been sanctioned

---

[27] "PM's Closing Remarks at the Chief Minister's Conference on Internal Security, New Delhi, December 20, 2007.

[28] The panel was constituted in May 2006. See the Report of the Planning Commission Expert Group on Development Challenges in Extremist Affected Areas, New Delhi: Planning Commission, April 2007.

and an amount of Rs. 10.50 cr has already been released.

CoBRA Battalions

Further, the MHA has decided in 2008 to carve out 10 battalions from the CRPF in order to create a specialised force to exclusively fight the Maoists. According to one account, these would be completely operational by 2013, where as the MHA said that they would be fully functional by 2011. These battalions would be established at a total cost of Rs 1389 cr — Rs 898.12 for infrastructure and Rs 491.35 for training.

Rationale: While analysing this tendency of a security-centric view of the Naxalite issue, one analyst wrote in 2007 that the "... 'militaristic approach' adopted by the Centre and state governments in assessing the field level situation, is perhaps extremely convenient to the ruling parties, since a military statistics-driven assessment would emphatically lead to planning on a military plane. The execution of development-oriented programmes is naturally placed at a secondary level"[29]. Thus, the successes of the government are assessed on the basis of numbers of rebels killed/arrested/ surrendered, or incidents of violence and exchange-of-fire, or numbers of weapons looted from the security forces/ recovered from the guerrillas.

Political Response

Political problem

The Maoist problem is essentially a political one. Yet, the Centre, or any of the affected States, is yet to admit this publicly. Beginning with treating the Maoist issue as an entirely law and order problem, the Centre has, subsequently, veered around to recognise that the movement has strong socio-economic underpinnings. One is not sure how long more the Centre might take to recognise and admit publicly that the issue has to be, indeed, addressed on a political plane. The Planning Commission's Expert Group observed in April 2008: "... the Naxalite movement has to be recognised as a political movement with a strong base among the landless and poor peasantry and adivasis.... Though its professed long-term ideology is

---

[29] K Srinivas Reddy, "The Maoist Challenge", Seminar, New Delhi, January 2007.

capturing state power by force, in its day to day manifestation it is to be looked upon as basically a fight for social justice, equality, protection and local development. The two have to be seen together without over playing the former... Since the goals of the movement are political it has to be addressed politically"[30].

Two Streams

There are two streams of arguments on the political response to the Maoists. The Planning Commission Expert Group and some analysts hold that the government cannot rule out the possibility of conducting negotiations with the rebels. But, the declared, present policy of the Centre is that there cannot be talks with the Maoists unless they abjure arms and violence.

From Charu to Ganapathy: Consistency

As Charu Mazumdar said, "Militant struggles must be carried on not for land, crops, etc., but for the seizure of State power". The Maoists of the present day, too, are equally clear and emphatic about it. In October 2004, on the occasion of the founding of the CPI-Maoist, its two top leaders — Ganapathy and Kishan — made a similar assertion: "The immediate aim and programme of the Maoist party is to carry on and complete the already ongoing and advancing New Democratic Revolution. This revolution will be carried out and completed through protracted people's war with the armed seizure of power remaining as its central and principal task."

Vacillation and Inconsistency

The Centre has categorically stated in its 14-point policy, unveiled on March 13, 2006, that 'there can be no peace talks with the Maoists unless they agree to abjure violence and arms'. Herein again, the Centre's lack of consistency and confusion in policy clearly comes to the fore. Speaking on the sidelines of the Conference of Chief Ministers of Naxalite affected States, the Home Minister said, on September 19, 2005, "If they drop arms, it is good. But if they want to carry arms and still talk... we have no problem".

---

[30] See the Report of the Planning Commission Expert Group, p. 51.

This vacillation continues even today. In an interview to a news agency on October 24, 2009, the Union Home Minster, while emphasising that the Centre had not set laying down arms as a pre-condition for holding talks with the Maoists, said, "I have not used these words. Besides I am too practical to know that they will not lay down arms. They have to halt violence which means halt the wanton destruction of railway track, roads, telephone towers, school buildings and bridges." He should have also advised, if not warned, the rebels to desist from brutal and cold-blooded killings of police personnel and innocent civilians who they often brand as police informers.

Three things stand out clearly. One, the MHA has moved significantly from its hard-line position. "We will talk, we will act, we will restore order and we will undertake developmental activities", the Home Minister said on August 17, while addressing the Chief Ministers Conference on Internal Security.

A month earlier, on July 7, answering a question in the Lok Sabha, the Home Minister said: "I am of the view and my Ministry is of the view that we would first have to clear and hold an area dominated by Naxalites and then developmental activities will take place. He went to elaborate that the rebels impeded development activities and programmes. "We build a road and they mine the road. We put a telephone tower and they blast the telephone tower. We build schools and panchayat houses, they blast them."

He, thus, while not entirely negating the two-pronged approach of maintaining law and order and initiating development activities, gave primacy to militarily dealing with the guerrillas before undertaking development activities in affected areas when he said: "Therefore, the State has to first gain total control over an area before actually development can take place." The Home Minister's October 30-statement, thus, indicates a significant departure from the earlier stand.

Two, the Home Minister's statements betray a sense of inconsistency and vacillation in the Centre's approach in dealing with the Maoists. Addressing a gathering in Mumbai, on October 7, the Home Minister said: "As long as the CPI (Maoist) believes in armed liberation struggle, we have no option but to ask our security forces to engage them…we will arrest them, we will apprehend them." This stands in stark contrast to what the Home Minister said over the past one week.

He reiterated the Centre's position on October 30: "They have to abjure violence and then we can work out the process [of talks] and we will advise the State governments to talk to them. But first they have to abjure violence".

Three, there is the possibility that the Maoists might misconstrue the Home Minister's appeal to them to 'give up' violence as a sign of 'helplessness', and then go about with their macabre acts of violence and wanton destruction.

Relevance of Revolutionary Politics

India's political leaders are yet to afford a convincing response to the Maoists' stand on people's problems[31]. The Maoists' arguments find resonance when they speak of the displacement, dispossession and unemployment of the people as a result of the government acquiring lands, especially those of the tribal population — in spite of specific regulations to the contrary such as Act 1/70 in Andhra Pradesh and the famous and "historic" Samata Judgement, to give them away to big industrial houses, including multi-national companies (MNCs), for a song. For the Maoists, political struggle is as important as the military struggle. Unpopular initiatives of the state, thus, feed into the Maoist propaganda. To counter this, the political leadership would need to reach out to the people, and prove that its actions were never meant to be anti-people.

As an analyst wrote, "… there is little effort by the political leadership to reassure society that a democratic polity can indeed provide effective solutions to the people's problems. Consequently, if even a minuscule section of society finds relevance in revolutionary politics, the blame squarely lies with the politician and administrator..."

---

[31] P.V. Ramana, "Trends in India's Maoist Movement", in SD Muni, ed, IDSA Asian Strategic Review 2008, (New Delhi: Academic Foundation, 2008)

Are Talks a Way Out?

The Planning Commission Expert Group and those who plead for talks with the rebels argue that the Centre cannot apply different yard sticks to different groups, and contends that when the government is prepared to hold talks with the United Liberated Front of Asom (ULFA), and has been holding peace negotiations with the Naga insurgents since nearly a decade.

On their part, the Maoists, too, have been rhetorical on the issue of talks. On-and-off they have expressed their intent to talk. At the same time, they have also clearly declared their intent to continue with their campaign of violence.

The Union Home Minister also acknowledged this when he said, "I regret to say that the response so far has been disappointing." CPI (Maoist) general secretary Muppala Lakshmana Rao alias Ganapathy declared on October 17, 2009, "We shall confront the new offensive of the enemy by stepping-up.... heroic resistance and preparing the entire party, PLGA [People's Liberation Guerrilla Army], the various revolutionary parties and organisations and the entire people."

The eventual question is: would the Maoists give up arms if their demands are met? And, what would be their demands? If the government accedes, the rebels would showcase it as their success in achieving something tangible for the people from a government that was hitherto reluctant to concede. If the government does fulfil their demands, on the other hand they would allege that the government has been insincere. This has been the experience in Andhra Pradesh in October 2004.

Response of Various affected States

On the other hand, the response of the various State governments, with the exception of Andhra Pradesh, has often, if not always, at best been found to be lagging and reactive.

Also, there is no unanimity in the perception of the various affected states on the Naxalite issue. Thus, while States such as Chhattisgarh and Tamil Nadu have proscribed the CPI (Maoist), West Bengal has refused to do the same. Orissa has lately proscribed the CPI (Maoist), while Karnataka issued contradictory statements and finally chose not to ban the CPI (Maoist).

On its part, Andhra Pradesh allowed the ban to lapse, initiated a peace process and re-imposed proscription in August 2005, in the wake of the assassination of a serving MLA in August 2005. It is pertinent to also point here that except for the CPI (Maoist) no other Naxalite group in the country has been proscribed in any of the states or by the Centre, even though some of them are committed to protracted armed struggle.

Further, coordination between the police and intelligence agencies of various affected States has been far from satisfactory. Presently, initial indications of a change in this trend are just about being witnessed, as was evidenced by the seizure of 875 empty rocket shells in September 2006. Also, towards end-August 2006 every single affected state has submitted its security and development plan for addressing the Naxalite issue. But, for the past many years thus far, the response by the various States has either been one of inaction, or focused in significant measure, if not excessively, on militarily fighting the Naxalites, rather than addressing the issue on a socio-economic plane.

Conclusion

The assertions by the MHA that the Maoist challenge could be dealt with in three years barely inspires any confidence. It is unlikely that the rebels and their challenge could be defeated in less than seven to 10 years. But, it is also heartening to note that there are signs of the various State governments and the Union government displaying the willingness to deal with the rebels head on and squarely address the issue. It would take some time to build consensus among all the affected States. Further, it would also take time to build the capacities of the police forces in the affected States.

Eventually, when the Union government and the various affected States weaken the Maoists, not by force alone, but through curtailing their violence as well as systematically reaching out the fruits of development to the remote and interior areas, rejuvenating the institutions of governance and re-occupying the space that it vacated and which the rebels have occupied, gradually, the people would be either won over or weaned away from the rebels. Then, the Maoists would be forced to wind-up shop honourably, or they would be cold-shouldered, if not driven away, by the people themselves.

Annex-I

SRE GUIDELINE, 2005

A. Criteria for inclusion of States under the SRE Scheme:

(i) Existence of and activities by one or more of the organizations (which have been declared unlawful associations/terrorist organizations either under the Unlawful Activities (Prevention) Act, 1967 or any other Act in the State);

(ii) Enactment of legislation by a State to tackle activities of naxal extremists or similar organizations;

(iii) Raising of India Reserve Battalions by the concerned States for curbing the activities of extremists; and

(iv) Inadequate development of affected areas due to hindrances created by extremist activities.

B. Criteria for inclusion of districts under the SRE scheme:

(i) Intensity of naxal violence over a period of five years. Exceptions can be made in some cases where it is found that a particular district which was earlier not affected or marginally affected, has, over the past two/three years, been reporting a large number of cases of naxal violence;

(ii) The organizational consolidation attained by the various naxal outfits in the affected district. Whether the districts are having 'Liberated area' or 'guerrilla zones' where the extremist outfit(s) virtually run a parallel administration even though the overall violence profile may not be very high;

(iii) The presence of armed dalams, their free movement and their fire power which would determine the potentiality of an extremist outfit to commit violent acts and be a serious threat to internal security. The sophistication in arms holding has to be a determining factor,

(iv) The spread of active mass front organizations of the naxal groups that lend constant and effective support in terms of logistics and safe refuge to the armed cadres, needs to be taken into consideration to judge the extent to which particular districts are affected; and

(v) Extent of pro-active measures initiated by the police/administration to counter the naxal extremists.

Source: Parliamentary Standing Committee on Home Affairs, *112th Report, Demands for Grants, 2005-2006*, New Delhi: Rajya Sabha Secretariat, April 2005.

RISE OF NAXALISM, ITS IMPLICATIONS FOR NATIONAL SECURITY AND THE WAY FORWARD *

E.N. Rammohan

"If the country does not belong to everyone it will belong to no one."

Tupamaro Manifesto

In any insurgency, the first step that the Government should take is to study the economic background of the movement, assess the causes and then dovetail the security strategy with the plan of setting right the economic, social and development failures. Economic and social injustices can be set right as the security operations progress. This paper is based on two factors i.e. security and delivering economic and social justice. When these are delivered the insurgency will wither leaving no cause for any of the affected people to fight with the government.

The best model of a counterinsurgency that succeeded was the campaign conducted by President Magsaysay of the Philippines against the Huk guerillas. Left-wing extremism or Naxalite insurgency in India strongly resembles the situation in the Philippines when the Huk insurgency erupted before the Second World War and continued after the country was given freedom by the United States. The main grievance in the Huk insurgency was land. Tenant farmers were being squeezed by big land holders and were getting a raw deal in tenancy rights. Regrettably the Government sided with the landlords and set the police and the military against the Huk guerillas. The police and the military committed excesses against the tenant

---

* Earlier published in USI Journal, Jan- March 2007. Reproduced with the permission of USI

farmers for supporting the guerillas. Magsaysay amended the tenancy laws in favour of the tenant farmers, reigned in his Army and ensured that no excesses were allowed to be committed. This changed the scenario and the Huk insurgency gradually withered away.

In India, the obstacles hindering the counter insurgency effort, can be easily identified. One is bad politics or rotten politics that Philippines did not have. The second is caste which is at the root of the Naxalite problem. The third problem is a peculiar concept that was introduced into the body politic and administration of India during the emergency and perpetuated thereafter by all political parties without exception. This is the concept of 'committed bureaucracy' not just to the party in power but to the family heading the party in power. When caste becomes conjoined with politics a stranglehold is created and the oppression of the economically poor communities continues with the denial of economic and social justice. The concept of committed bureaucracy protects the perpetrators of oppression against lower castes. These people are then motivated by the left-wing extremist parties.

The following paragraphs examine the incidents of left-wing extremism in India briefly, assessing the cause of violence.

1946- The Tebhaga Movement in Undivided Bengal

This movement demanded that the share of the landlords be reduced from one half to one third. The movement spread from Rangpur and Dinajpur in the north to 24 Parganas in the south. When their demands were not heard, the Kisan Sabhas, dominated by the Communist party, encouraged peasants to forcibly take two-thirds of the harvested crop from granaries. This resulted in bloody clashes between the peasants and the landlords. However, the movement petered out with the repression of the landlords and the local administration.

1946-51- The Telengana Insurrection

This movement was directed by the Communists. Peasants launched their struggle against economic issues against forced labour, illegal exactions and unauthorised evictions. It soon developed into an uprising against the feudal rule of the Nizam. More than 4000 lives were lost before the Communist party withdrew the struggle. The Telengana insurrection (1946-51) was broad-based and had no parallel in Indian History since the 1857 Sepoy Mutiny.

1967- Naxalbari

This revolt took place in the area of three police stations-Naxalbari, Kharibari and Phansidewa. About 65% of the population around these three police stations was scheduled castes and tribals.They worked as agricultural labourers or in mines, forests and plantations. A small percentage owned small holdings. The majority cultivated on agency basis (baghchash). The baghchashis were exploited by the jotedars. When the land reforms act was passed in 1955, the jotedars started malafide transfers of land. Santhals armed with bows and arrows forcibly occupied the lands of the kulaks, lifted stocks of hoarded rice and killed an Inspector of police. Thereafter there were a number of such incidents. This followed a major deployment of police forces by the CPI (M) government and after several operations the movement was squashed. The leadership of the movement comprised communist cadres who were following the path set by Mao Tse Tung after the Cultural Revolution. This culminated in the formation of the Communist Party of India Marxist-Leninist (CPI-ML) on 22 April 1969. Even though not more than a score of people were killed in this uprising, it left a far reaching impact on the entire agrarian scene throughout India. This effect can be compared to the several ripples that a single pebble can create in water.

1968- Srikakulam

Girijans or tribals comprised about 70% of the population of Srikakulam district living in the agency area of the Eastern Ghats. They were mainly involved in agriculture, while some collected minor forest produce. The British, conscious that they may be harassed by the plainsmen decreed that no land could be transferred from a Girijan to a plainsman without the permission of the District Collector. The Act was unfortunately observed more in the breach. The traders and money lenders took full advantage of the poverty of the Girijans. They supplied their daily requirements like tobacco, kerosene, salt and cloth on credit and also lent money for purchase of seeds. Those unable to clear their debts were made to part with their land. Thus, most of the fertile land passed into the hands of the plainsmen. The landlords squeezed them to the utmost and paid subsistence wages. Lease holders had to give two-thirds of their produce to the landlord. It was in 1967 that Vempatapu Satyanarayana started work amongst the Girijans. The movement he led was able to make substantial gains for the poor Girijans. Wages of farm servants rose, the landlord's share of harvest was reduced from 2/3 to 1/3, 2000 acres of land was wrested from the landlords and more than 5000 acres of wasteland came under the possession of Girijans. Later on 31 October 1967 a clash took place between a large group of tribals who were bound for a meeting of the Marxist party and a group of landlords. The landlord group had guns and they shot and killed two tribals. The Girijans were incensed and the movement became violent. Vempatapu Satyararayana organized the Girijans into guerilla squads called Dalams. At this stage, the Srikakulam leadership who had joined the CPI (M) faction of the Communist party broke away from the CPI (M) and joined a group that split from it to form the All India Coordination Committee of Communist Revolutionaries which in due course evolved into the Communist Party of India, Marxist–Leninist CPI (ML). There were a series of raids on houses of landlords and money lenders; their houses were burnt down and cash was looted. There were a number of encounters with the police. From December 1968 to January 1969, twenty nine policemen were killed in action by the Dalams. Charu Mazumdar, the CPI (ML) leader visited Srikakulam and gave a fillip to the movement. During 1969 the Naxalites committed 23 murders and 40 dacoities. Some of the murders were gruesome. For example, on 11 May 1969, a landlord, P. Jammu Naidu of Ethamanuguda was killed and slogans were painted with his blood by the members of the Dalam that executed him. He was notorious for grabbing land from the poor tribals and forcibly taking their daughters as his wives. When he was killed he had seven wives, two of whom were little girls he had forcibly taken from tribals. This showed the extent of exploitation of the tribal people by the upper caste landlords. The extent of the exploitation of the forest tribals who collected minor forest produce is evident in an account of a trial of a sahukar by a Peoples Court. The sahukar or usurer used to go into the Agency area to collect tamarind from the forest Girijans. The list of borrowers which he brought showed that he had lent a sum of Rs. 280/- to peasants of 4 villages. Against this he proposed to collect from them 40 bundles of tamarinds which at the market rate was worth Rs. 1600/-. This meant that the peasants were to pay back nearly six Rupees for every Rupee they had borrowed! The usurer was arrested and tried before a Peoples Court. He repented and promised to behave and not fleece the peasants.

1967-71-West Bengal, Midnapur and Birbhum

The Midnapur district of West Bengal bordering Bihar and Orissa witnessed a well planned and well organized Naxalite movement in the Debra and Gopibhallavpur police stations. The district has a sizeable tribal population of Santhals, Oraons and Lodhas. The majority of them were landless labourers. A small proportion owned small plots of land or cultivated the jotedar's land under the Barga system. Gopibhallavpur has a long forested border with Orissa and Bihar. After the Naxalbari uprising in 1967, a section of CPI (M) workers in Midnapur started propagating the extremist line. They supported the kisans and bargadars and worked for a movement against the jotedars. Santosh Rana, Ashim Mukherjee, both first class postgraduates of Calcutta University and a host of students from well to do upper caste families from Calcutta lived and worked among the tribals, identifying themselves wholeheartedly with them. From September 1969, big tribal groups armed with spears, bows and arrows attacked the houses of jotedars killed some of them, looted cash and burnt all deeds of land. The State Government alarmed at the spate of killings sent several companies of CRPF and state police and by March 1970, the area was brought under control. The Naxalite uprising in Birbhum district was also masterminded by several students from Calcutta University. The State Government reacted by deputing CRPF, State Armed Police companies and an Army infantry company for cordoning and searching the area. Nearly 150 CPI (ML) cadres were arrested and the movement died down.

1968-70 -Bihar and Uttar Pradesh

The Mushahari block of Muzaffarpur district of Bihar covers 12 villages with a population of about 10,000 people. There were various forms of oppression by the upper class on the peasantry. In April 1968, the peasants of Gangapur harvested the arahar crop of the landlord in broad daylight. Retaliation was quick. Bijli Singh the zamindar of Narsingpur organized an attack on the peasants with 300 men armed with lathis, swords and firearms with the landlord leading on an elephant. In the fight that ensued, the landlord and his hoodlums were routed. The humbling of this powerful landlord by the harijan peasants had a magical effect on the surrounding villages.

Kisan Sangram Samitis were formed and there were incidents of seizing of land by the peasants. In April 1969, landless peasants forcibly harvested the crop on 14 acres of land of a landlord. There was a clash in which the retainer of the landlord was killed. In June 1969, an attack was made in Paharchat village. The landlord and two associates were killed. Hundreds of peasants gathered after the raid. In their presence all the deeds and documents were burnt and the pawned ornaments returned to the owners. This was followed by a series of similar events. Alarmed, the State sent police forces and after several combing operations, the movement died down. The Mushahari struggle caused ripples to spread into Dharbangha, Champaran and Chota Nagpur. Here in May 1970, 54 Adivasis were arrested in the Jaduguda forest during police operations. Mary Tyler, a British national was among them. Later she wrote poignantly about the movement-"The Naxalites crime was the crime of all those who cannot remain unmoved and inactive in an India where a child crawls in the dust with a begging bowl, where a poor girl can be sold as a rich man's plaything, where an old woman must half starve herself in order to buy social acceptance from the powers that be in her village; where countless people die of sheer neglect, where many are hungry while food is hoarded for profit, where usurers and tricksters extort the fruits of labour from those who do the work, where the honest suffer, while the villainous prosper, where justice is the exception and injustice the rule and where the total physical and mental energy of millions of people is spent on the struggle for mere survival."[1]

The Naxalite violence that erupted in Singhbum and Ranchi had more serious dimensions. Jamshedpur became a mini Calcutta, with instances of attacks on schools and, government offices and police piquets. Schools were also attacked in Jamshedpur. There were also large scale attacks in Ranchi. In Uttar Pradesh, the Palia area is part of the Lakhimpur district in the Terai region. It was inhabited by Tharu tribals. The state government encouraged poor peasants to go to the Palia area, allotting 10-12 acres of land to each family. The landlords had forcibly occupied big chunks of land, ejecting the poor peasants. This provided the Naxalites with fertile ground for agitation. Their object was to clear the area of big farmers, thugs, corrupt political leaders and moneylenders.[2] A series of attacks and raids on landlords ensued, in which a number of firearms were also snatched. Deployment of the armed police in the area brought the situation under control.

In all these states the Naxalite movements were organized and coordinated by various CPI (ML) groups. Unfortunately the top Marxist-Leninist leaders like Charu Mazumdar in West Bengal, Satyanarain Singh of Bihar, were not tactically sound in their approach. They thought that there would be mass uprisings and they could build up a Peoples Liberation Army from the rag-tag band of peasants who had revolted against the atrocities of landlords and money lenders. Charu Mazumdar succeeded in arousing the students of Calcutta who left their studies to live in the forest villages and share the tribulations of the tribals. The vital element of building up a guerilla force and training and equipping them to take on the might of the state was lacking. One by one the movements fizzled out as the Paramilitary forces with the State Police were deployed in the interior areas and well planned raids and search operations were carried out. The CPI (ML) leadership lacked the vision to organize the poor peasants against the might of the state, though the cause was just. Also, lumpen elements infiltrated the leftist groups and affected the discipline of the groups.

---

[1] Mary Tyler, My Years in an Indian Prison, (London: Gollancz, 1977), p-191.

[2] Prakash Singh, The Naxalite Movement in India (New Delhi: Rupa, 2006), p72.

According to a rough estimate there were about 4000 incidents of Naxalite violence from the middle of 1970 to the middle of 1971, with 3500 in West Bengal, 220 in Bihar and 70 in Andhra Pradesh. The Government of India made a plan for joint operations in West Bengal, Bihar and Orissa with the Army, Paramilitary forces and the State Police. This operation was undertaken from 1 July to 15 August 1971.This was Operation Steeplechase. The broad strategy was to surround an area that was a known stronghold with an outer cordon of the Army, an inner cordon of the CRPF, and local police operating inside. The operation disrupted the network of the naxalite cadres and the movement stalled. Meanwhile internal dissensions between the factions of the CPI (ML) also disrupted the movement. A number of top leaders were arrested, including Charu Mazumdar. When he died shortly after, it marked the end of a phase of the Naxalite movement in India. However, it was only a lull. The movement was to surface again, for the Indian Government had not removed the causes of the insurgency. This movement was not going to be finished with cosmetic remedies. The causes were deep rooted in caste, the crucial factor behind the exploitation of the poor and the downtrodden.

1980- Peoples War Group (PWG) Andhra Pradesh, Madhya Pradesh and Maharashtra

Andhra Pradesh has a radical tradition going back to the Telengana struggle of 1946-51. The Girijan awakening in Srikakulam had preceded the Naxalite movement. The forces of the state squelched the uprising by 1970. The movement however continued to simmer. After Charu Mazumdar's death, his associates Kondapalli Seetharamiah, KG Satyamurthy and Suniti Kumar Ghosh formed a Central Organising Committee in December 1972, concentrating on organizing and mobilizing the masses. They decided to eschew militancy until such time as the party was strong enough to embark on a course of violence. Kondapalli Seetharamiah encouraged the party workers to 'commit money actions' an euphemism for dacoity or robbery. He was arrested on 26 April 1977, but jumped bail and thereafter organized underground activities on a large scale. He broke away from the COC CPI (ML) on 20 April 1980 and formed the CPI (ML) Peoples War Group. For the next ten years he moved from strength to strength and the Peoples War Group emerged as the most formidable Naxalite formation in the country.[3]

What led to the resurgence of Naxalism in the Telengana area? The basic reason was the continued economic exploitation of the tribals by the landlords, traders and government officials especially those of the Forest Department. As P.S. Sundaram wrote-"The tribals owning small pieces of land are expropriated and sharecroppers impoverished. They are all kept under perpetual bondage towards repayment of a small debt supposedly taken generations ago. The forest wealth is freely smuggled out by contractors in connivance with the forest staff. The tribals get neither a remunerative price for their produce nor a fair wage for their labour."[4]

The social dimensions of exploitation were far more revolting. The landlords of the region were commonly known as Dora (lord). C. Lokeswara Rao has described the high-handedness of the Doras, the tyranny of Doras in Telengana is unmatched. Tribal girls working on the Dora's land are forcibly taken in his household and are at the disposal of the master and his guests. She is forced to have abortions when she gets pregnant. She has to subsist on the leftovers passed on by the cook, but has to satisfy the appetite of just about any male in the master's household. Naxalite songs are replete with references to rape by landlords and to girls growing up with the knowledge of the inevitability of rape that awaits them. Only a few such practices have disappeared and the pace of change is slow.

On 20 May 1981, the Naxalites had called for a meeting of tribals at Indraveli in Adilabad district. More than 30,000 tribals had turned up. The administration refused permission for the meeting, apprehending a clash between landlords and tribals, however the tribals were determined to have the meeting. There was a lathi charge and firing and 13 Gond tribals were killed. The PWG exploited the anger of the tribals and consolidated their hold on the area. Kondapalli Seetharamiah was arrested for the second time on 2 January 1982 but escaped from hospital on 4 January 1984. He now

---

[3] Ibid, p-130.

[4] Causes of Spurt in Naxalite Violence. Indian Express. 1 September 1987.

concentrated on organization of the PWG cadres and constituted Forest Committees for the forest areas and Regional Committees for the plains areas. Armed squads or dalams comprising 6 to 10 members were formed and about 50 dalams were soon active in Telengana.

The PWG is believed to have redistributed nearly half a million acres across Andhra Pradesh. The modus operandi was to forcibly occupy excess land of big land owners and give them away to the landless or to the labourers working for the landlord. As per the State Government's own admission, counter affidavit 68/82 filed by the state against the Naxalites, the radicals had forcibly redistributed 80,000 acres of agricultural land and 20,000 acres of forest land. What was the government doing all this time since the land ceiling act came into being? This is the crux of the matter in Andhra Pradesh and in many states of India where the Land Ceiling Act is not enforced. Party activists insisted on a hike in the daily minimum wages from Rs. 15/- to Rs. 25/- and the annual fee for jeetagadu (year long labour) from Rs. 2000/- to Rs. 4000/-.[5] The poorer sections were particularly happy at these two measures but found that this can be turned into reality only with the intervention of the Naxalites. Gorakala Doras (Lord of the Bushes) is how the Naxalites came to be known in the interior forest areas.

Revolutionary writers helped in furthering the Naxalite ideology. The moving spirit of the Jana Natya Mandali, the cultural front of the PWG was Gummadi Vittal Rao, better known as Gaddar. This wandering minstrel's ballads inspired the simple tribal. He became a legend in Andhra Pradesh.

The PWG fought successive battle with the Telugu Desam Government. When the Congress came to power in 1989 they were soft on the Naxalites and freed many of them under detention and in prison. They however did nothing to control the exploitation of the tribals like enforcing the land ceiling or controlling the moneylenders. The Naxalites began organizing, extorting money and running peoples courts, giving the general impression of a parallel government. As a result, Congress resumed their hard-line strategy.

---

[5] Chidananda Rajghatta, "Madiga Malliah Inherits the Earth", The Times of India. 9 December 1990.

Soon the PWG had spread to the adjoining areas of Maharashtra, Madhya Pradesh, and Orissa and into some areas of Tamil Nadu and Karnataka. They also acquired 50-60 AK 47 rifles, probably from the LTTE. Naxalite violence gradually stepped up and peaked in 1991 with several attacks on railway and electrical installations, police stations and patrols. On 8 May 1992, the PWG was banned and coordinated operations commenced against them by the central Paramilitary forces and the State Police. The operation was successful with 3500 cadres arrested and 8500 surrendering. By 1993, the Naxalites surged back with rising violence.

They now spread to the Bastar district of Madhya Pradesh, which till then was a sleepy forest outpost. The tribals of Bastar were used to a life of deprivation. They made the truant teacher to take classes regularly and the absentee doctor to attend to his patients. This made the tribals look at the Naxalite cadres with awe and respect. Writing about Bastar the Peoples Union of Civil liberties explained that a lopsided socio-economic development of the district caused by exploitation through cheating and duping was an ideal setting for the Naxalites to take root in the area. With their idealism, free of corruption or other vested interests, they could win the confidence of the tribals. They even punished corrupt officials and made the tendu leaf contractors increase the wages.[6] The movement spread to Balaghat and Rajnandgaon districts.

Gadchiroli district of Maharashtra is largely inhabited by tribals. The jungle is spread through 10,495 square kilometers out of the district area of 15,434 square kilometres. The entire life of the tribals revolves around the forests, yet the tribals were denied access to the forests due to the obtuse interpretation of the Forest Act and rules. With the coming of the Naxalites, the forest officials abdicated their jurisdiction. The best testimonial of the presence of the Naxalites was given by an innocent tribal who got a lift from the Commissioner of Scheduled castes and tribes during his visit in Gadchiroli district. The Naxalites are called Dadas in Gadchiroli. When asked about the Dadas, the tribal replied- "There is at least one change since the Dadas have come. The government atrocities are over and the

---

[6] The Illustrated Weekly of India. 3 September 1989.

police cannot harass us."[7] There were 113 incidents of Naxalite violence in the district in 1990 with 16 deaths. On 12 November 1991, ten CRPF personnel were killed and 13 injured in a landmine explosion under their vehicle. The PWG has attained a high degree of expertise in making and detonating improvised explosive devices (IED).

The New Left in Bihar

The best description of the dismal state of affairs in Bihar is summed up by Arvind N Das- "Bihar's economy has been at a stand still for decades. The discriminatory nature of public and private investments, the green revolution bypassing the state, principally on account of non-implementation of land reforms, the willful subversion of whatever social security system existed, all these has pushed the people into poverty, the economy into backwardness, the society into violence."[8] The resentment of the oppressed sections in this environment found an outlet in the emergence of a 'New Left' manifested in the form of three Naxalite groups in the beginning of 1980- The Maoist Communist Centre (MCC), CPI ML (Anti Lin Biao Group) and the CPI-ML Party Unity. In May 1982, the Bihar Government reported that 47 out of the 857 blocks were affected by the Naxalite movement. Subsequently the movement has grown enormously in the face of a corrupt, casteist and incompetent administration.[9] When the CPI-ML was formed, one Naxalite group Dakshin Desh had remained aloof. Amulya Sen and Kanai Chatterjee were its leaders. They considered mass mobilisation as a precursor to armed action. The group chose Jangal Mahal area of Burdwan, with a sizeable population of scheduled castes and tribals, for its operations. Agricultural land was inadequate, irrigation virtually nonexistent, and the wage rates dismally low, all conditions suitable for a Naxalite uprising. The landlords generally belonged to the upper castes, while the sharecroppers and landless labour were scheduled castes or tribals, providing the ideal mix for the Naxalites to enter. By 1973, the party had 37 militias who organized actions

---

[7] Commissioner for Schedules Caste and Scheduled Tribes, 29th Report, 1987-89, Government of India, p-171

[8] Arvind N. Das, The Republic of Bihar. (New Delhi: Penguin, 1992), p-14.

[9] Ibid, p- 107.

like looting of food grains, killing of class enemies and snatching of arms.

In 1975, the group was renamed as the Maoist Communist Centre (MCC). The MCC gradually spread over Central Bihar. Its membership exceeded 10,000 and they had stockpiled about 700 weapons including some AK rifles. There were gruesome slaughters of Rajputs by Yadavs in the MCC. These were more in the form of feuds between the two communities and mainly because of the way the Rajputs treated the Yadavs. On 29 May 1987 the Yadav cadres of the MCC slaughtered 42 Rajputs of Baghaura and Dalelchak villages of Aurangabad district. On 12 February 1992, 37 members of the landowning Bumihar caste were hacked to death by the MCC cadres in Bara village of Gaya district.

Vinod Misra formed the CPI-ML anti Lin Biao faction in December 1973. It struck roots in Bhojpur district and spread to Rohtas, Jehanabad, Patna and Nalanda districts. They had 50 underground armed squads and weapons, mostly country made guns, a few rifles and sten guns. The Indian Peoples Front was the political front of the anti Lin Biao faction.

The CPI (ML) Party Unity was formed in 1982 by the merger of the COC CPI (ML) of Andhra and the Unity Organization of CPI-ML of West Bengal. The Party Unity has about 30,000 members. It has 25 armed squads holding about 150 weapons, including a few sten guns.

The third phase of Naxalite violence commenced with the holding of the 9th Congress of the Peoples War Group in 2001 in which it was decided to arm the Peoples Guerilla Army with more sophisticated weapons. This phase extended the Naxalite war to nine states.

The Salwa Judum of Chhattisgarh

The case of the exploitation of the adivasis of Bastar is a little different from the similar cases in Andhra Pradesh, West Bengal, Bihar and even Maharashtra. The area affected in Madhya Pradesh borders Telengana and Srikakulam and also Koraput in Orissa. The adivasis are much simpler than their counterparts in the other states mentioned. When Andhra Pradesh established the Greyhound Force, a counter insurgency force with the help of a retired Security Service Bureau officer in 1989, the quality of the counterinsurgency operations improved and the leftist guerillas found themselves at the receiving end. Encounters forced them to retreat into Bastar and Koraput, where they found their brother adivasis much more meek and tolerant of the oppression by the caste Hindu landlords and the banias. The problem here was less with exploitation on land and much more with the sale of forest produce. The hardened guerillas of Andhra found their brother adivasis too timid to arouse and join forces with them against the oppressors. At this point they made a mistake and tried to intimidate the adivasis of Madhya Pradesh and coerce them to join their groups. This 'Press Ganging' alienated many of the local adhivasis and they began to look for help in the district authorities. It was at this point that some local adivasi leaders who were in politics and the local civil bureaucrats and police officers got the idea of resettling the forest dwelling adivasis in areas where some control could be exercised over them. This has gravitated into forcing many forest dwellers to leave their huts and come and live in settlements nearer the towns. Sudeep Chakaravarthi traveling in the area was aghast to see the miserable conditions of these forest dwellers living in dirt and squalor in miserable shanties. In many cases the police and civil bureaucracy had forced the forest dwelling families to burn their huts in forest glades and come and live in the settlements.[10]

Madhya Pradesh has meanwhile been divided and Bastar and Dandakarnya forests are now in Chattisgarh. This concept of resettling forest dwelling adivasis is the worst step that a professional fighting an insurgency would take. It is worse than the regrouping of villages done in the Naga Hills and Mizo Hill districts. The Nagas and Mizos have not forgotten the scars of that terrible period. There was one saving grace in that resettlement was that the politicians were not involved. In the Salwa Judum, the lead role is of the politician.

---

[10] Sudeep Chakravarti, "Red Sun- Travels in Naxalite Country", (New Delhi: Penguin, 2008)

Conclusion

In all the theatres of Naxalite violence, there has been a diagnostic response only in one state-West Bengal. Here the CPM government carried out Operation Barga under which sharecroppers were registered and given permanent and inheritable rights on cultivation of their plots covering a total area of 11 lakh acres. Besides, 1.37 lakh acres of ceiling surplus and benami lands were acquired by the state government and distributed among 25 lakh landless and marginal cultivators. The land reforms saw the emergence of a new class loosely termed 'rural rich' which weakened the social and political power enjoyed by the landlords in the countryside. In Andhra Pradesh, or Bihar the Land Ceiling Act has not been enforced even after more than 50 years of its legislation. There is much more that can be pointed to in the states of Andhra Pradesh and Bihar. The Law enforcing officers openly support the idea that the Naxalites are a band of thugs and criminals and must be wiped out. With this there is no question of the Land Ceiling being enforced. What they have left unsaid is that it is the right of the upper classes to have hundreds of acres of land and it is the duty of the scheduled classes and tribes to toil on these lands for the benefit of the upper classes. In this regard, the case of land tenancy in Kerala is of interest. The upper classes in Kerala were generally landlords but with medium holdings. The majority of the landlords had tenant farmers on their lands who deposited half of the crop to their landlords. The landlords themselves and their progeny were educated and took up white collar jobs in the metropolises of the country. When the CPI M was elected in the late fifties, they brought in land tenancy laws which accorded land ownership of the tenant holdings to those tenants who held tenancy for 12 years. At one stroke hundreds of upper caste landlords lost their holdings and tenant farmers got ownership rights of the lands that they had tilled for long years. This is one reason why the Naxalite movement could not grow its roots in Kerala.

The issue in the forest lands of Andhra Pradesh, Maharashtra, Madhya Pradesh, Chattisgarh and Jharkhand is different. Traditionally the forests here have been the home of the tribals for centuries. Here again the root cause is the caste factor. It is the Vaisya who trades and it is he who is the moneylender. In the forests of all the Naxalite affected states, the Bania has had a vice-like grip on the tribals. He lends money to them and collects minor forest produce against the loans, taking care that the tribal is perpetually indebted.

When posted in Hyderabad in 1989, I had chance to discuss the Naxalite problem with the state's Revenue Minister, who asked me how this problem could be solved? When I replied- "You have to enforce the Land Ceiling." The Revenue Minister of the state raised his hands and replied- "But that is impossible." What he did not tell me was that the two major castes of Andhra, the Reddys and the Kammas, both landlords would never allow the land ceiling to be enforced and that they were the main political forces in the state.

Here then is the crux of the problem. The same situation exists in Bihar, where the Brahmin, Bumihar and Rajput would rather have his land holdings in the names of his pet dogs and cats rather than allow the land ceiling to be enforced.

In the forests it is the bania, the Vaisya, who is in league with the political class and who bribes the bureaucrat and keeps the poor low castes and the tribals in perpetual subservience.There can be no solution to the problem of the CPI ML leading a proletariat rebellion without solving the basic problem of giving rights to the lower castes and the tribals and putting an end to the exploitation by the upper castes. Measures like the Salwa Judum are clever ploys by the same upper caste political and bureaucrat nexus operating. Above all there can be no military solution to this problem.

The Way Forward

The first step is to enforce the land ceiling. This has to be done forgetting the political factor of particular political parties wanting to retain power in states like Andhra Pradesh and Bihar. The Central Paramilitary Forces and the State Police which are used in operations against the Naxalites should be used to enforce the land ceiling, evict the landlords from their excessive holdings and ensure that the surplus lands are cultivated by the lowest classes and tribals. They should ensure that the new land holders and their harvest is secure. Once this is done the Naxalite cadres will not use landmines on the police forces.

In the forest tracts, laws should be enforced to the effect that only forest dwelling tribes and scheduled castes have access to forest lands. Upper castes should be prevented from entering the forests. Cooperatives should be established for tribals who can be trained and only these tribal cooperatives should be allowed to trade in forest produce. Branches of banks with micro credit loans as operated by the Grameen bank in Bangladesh should be set up with forest cooperatives to sanction loans for the forest tribes. The Paramilitary forces that were used to hunt the Naxalites should now be used to enforce the new laws for the forests. They should ensure that the bania does not enter within 100 kilometers of a forest, that all trade is carried out only by the Forest Cooperatives and that the branches of the micro credit Grameen banks are well guarded. With this the confidence levels of the tribals in the police forces and other government authorities may increase tremendously and will serve to wither the Naxalite movement.

Another pressing issue is that of the forest dwelling adhivasis and the discovery of minerals in these parts. The question is that of the ownership of these minerals. The Government, both State and Central and all the political parties, save the CPI Maoist say that the minerals belong to the Government and they have the right to sign a Memorandum of Understanding with any Company, Indian or Foreign to mine the minerals. The CPI Maoist and the Adivasis who have been organized by them assert that the minerals, in the forest where they have lived for centuries, belong to them and only they hold the decisive authority regarding mining. Going by the history of exploitation of the Scheduled Castes and Tribes by the upper Castes for thousands of years it is clear that minerals in a forest belong to the Adivasis who were dwelling in that forest for thousands of years. This can be further buttressed by similarities among the Red Indians in the United States and Aborigines in Australia.

Is it not imperative that we do as the Americans and Australians do in their respective Countries?

THE TRIBAL WAY OF LIFE: SECURITY OVER JUSTICE

Sharanya Nayak and Malini Subramaniam

*"Tribals will be happier left alone in the grandeur and freedom of the hills....
They lack many amenities of life. But they are free. No one interferes with
them and they are able to live as per their religion and tradition....What
greater happiness is there than in cultivating one's own fields? Why not let
them do so?"[1]* asked Verrier Elwin, one of the best known British Social
Anthropologist who spent 37 years living with the tribals in Central India
to understand them.

The post-modern Indian government has left neither the tribals alone
nor have they left their hills intact for them to freely bask around their hills.
The Bailadila Hills has been one of the first casualties of development while
the more recent Niyamgiri Hills is struggling to retain its 'grandeur' to keep
alive the faith of thousands of Dongria Kondhs.

At the centre stage of discussion today is not whether the hills and
forest should continue to face the guillotine at the altar of development or
whether the 8.4 million tribal people in India comprising some 648 distinct
communities (with 75 PTGs)[2] are reaping the benefits of 'development'
in an India that boasts of 'inclusive growth' but rather how can the tribal

---

[1] Verrier Elwin, A Philosophy of NEFA (North East Frontier Agency), (Assam: P. C. Dutta on
behalf of the Adviser to the Governor of Assam]; 2nd edition, 1964), 1

[2] Particularly Vulnerable Groups (PTGs) (earlier referred to as Primitive Tribal groups) are so
classified based on their pre-agricultural level of technology, very low level of literacy, and
declining or stagnant population.

communities be 'contained' from being influenced by an ideology as alien as Maoism. And that to undertake such a measure how best to ensure 'security', to what extent can military and para-military forces be sent into the forests to keep a check on the ideological 'indoctrination'? Is it not important to understand what discontent has driven the peace-loving community such as the tribals that derive its very essence of life from nature to draw its strength from an arm-wielding Maoist? Or has the Indian government fooled itself to believe that a largely illiterate, emaciated, half clad tribal men and women could simply be driven over or driven away to make way for 'development' that they see no sense in? What sense can development have to those who are indiscriminately uprooted from their culture, tradition, livelihood and their very sense of dignity?

The answers to these and many more questions that agitate many are difficult to find unless the very ethos of tribal way of life is understood and empathized with. It is equally important to understand the genesis of this betrayal, disappointment and discontent felt by tribal men and women that their vacant stares seem to convey when their life and their being is fixed in frames to accompany the frequent write-ups by one and many.

Tribal Way of Life: Making their Presence Felt

The advise that the tribal communities be left 'isolated' with scant attempt at 'governing' them comes from the historical lessons of tribal uprise and revolt to external intrusion. In fact history shows that whilst the tribal communities were very hospitable to the 'outsiders', any interference in their cultural belief system and traditional way of life associated with nature – jal, jungle, jameen (water, forest, land) has met with the fiercest of revolt.

Rampachodavaram rebellion of 1879 against the British and the non-tribals in Bastar by Dorlas and Koyas was sparked off by the colonial restrictions to access over forests and penalization of liquor brewing. The Bastar rebellion of 1910 led by Gunda Dhur, legendary Dhurua tribal leader revered as god in Bastar, was against the British Government's attempt at banning and penalizing *podu* or shifting cultivation, against the practice of *begar* or free bonded labour for landlords and against eviction from and access to forests. This was followed by Paderu rebellion of 1922-23 by the Koyas, the Parajas and the Kandha tribals led by legendary non-tribal revolutionary Alluri Sitaram Raju, who dons the walls of every rural home and urban street in Northern Andhra Pradesh. Sitaram Raju led the tribals in revolt against the colonial Government's banning and penalizing of *podu* and eviction of tribal settlements inside dense forests. A notable fact of this rebellion was that Raju led a guerrilla combat against the British, the first time that tribals were introduced to this kind of resistance.

During the same time as Sitaram Raju-led rebellion, there were simultaneous tribal uprisings in undivided Koraput (Orissa), undivided Bastar (Chhattisgarh) and the Munda-Oraon-Santhal-dominated areas of Jharkhand against the introduction and demarcation of vast tracts of virgin tribal forestlands as 'reserve forests'. We all remember Birsa Munda who fought to his last breath to save the forests of Khunti and forced the British to pass the *khut kati* laws or the Santhal Parganas and Chhota Nagpur Tenancy Acts. It was perhaps in the 1920s that the first forest surveys were carried out in the tribal areas of Bastar and Koraput and tribals forcefully evicted from their forest habitats. It is significant to note that simultaneous to creation of reserve forests was the entry of 'pardesis' or the non-tribals and most often upper or middle caste cultivators. In 1940 Gond and Kolam tribals of Adilabad in Northern Andhra Pradesh rose in revolt against the British led by Komra Bhimu against banning and penalizing of *podu*, eviction of tribals from reserves forests and settlement of non-tribal cultivators on tribal lands. In fact the first demands for comprehensive land settlement in favour of tribals were made during this rebellion by Komra Bhimu but obviously none heard him as he was a 'rebel without a cause' out to destroy the might of the British Empire.

However, it must be mentioned that other than the above revolts there have been several major revolts against the British as part of the Indian freedom movement by tribal icons like Saheed Laxman Naik. All the above revolts by tribals have been in response to attempts at controlling their resources and undermining their political powers over their regions. Thus any attempt at control has been resisted by tribals, whether in the pre-colonial feudal times, the colonial times or the present capitalist times. Predictably, the responses to tribal revolts have been to use greater counter-force to crush these revolts in order to devaluate the importance and profundity of what the tribals were conveying through resistance. It is a misfortune that neither then nor now the Government understands the causes of any tribal rebellion. Each revolt points to the fact that the tribal way of life was being undermined and that would not go down well with the tribals and they would only settle for greater autonomy and dignity. Tribals have communicated through their rebellions that their way of life revolves around their control over resources and freedom to govern their people on their own principles.

Colonial Response

The colonial rulers did begin to understand the exclusive nature of the tribal community and recognized early enough that their ethoses need to be respected. Thereby they enacted the Scheduled District Act of 1874 that enabled seclusion of tribal dominated areas protecting them from the generic rule applied to the rest of the country. However, way before the enactment of this act, the introduction of the land revenue system, such as the Permanent Settlement Act of 1793, Ryotwari System of 1792 and Mahalwari System of 1833 had done enough harm. In order to maximise tax revenues and simplify collection, the colonial state promoted settled agriculture as the preferred form of economic activity, and gradually obstructed a range of other material practices such as shifting cultivation and transhumant pastoralism. It made way for the oppressing moneylenders and in tribal dominated areas a series of tribal revolt was unleashed. It is estimated that about 70 tribal revolts took place over a period of 70 years (1778-1948). These revolts had a lot to do with the restrictions placed on access and control over forests by the colonial state with the enactment of the Indian Forest Acts of 1867, 1878 and 1927 and the Madras Forest Act 1882 that provided the legal basis for reservation of forests and 'settlement' and notification of forest rights[3]

---

[3] O.Springate-Baginski et.al., "Redressing 'historical injustice' through the Indian Forest Rights Act 2006: A Historical Institutional Analysis of Contemporary Forest Rights Reforms", IPPG Discussion Paper No.27, August 2009, URL: http://www.ippg.org.uk/papers/dp27.pdf, accessed on 4 September 2009

Their approach of being protective enshrined in the policy of 'leave them alone' did treat tribal areas as independent territories inhabited by autonomous communities. Ironically one cannot miss the free hand provided to missionaries to set up schools and religious centres that invaded tribal culture, language, religion and their very way of living. Later joined by Hindu missionaries, both these religious groups went about 'humanising' a community that practices human sacrifice and witchcraft, a rather 'rude, uncivilized, alcoholic, shunning contact with the external world yet with few wants and honest' lot. These were reasons enough to take them along 'in the march of civilization'. The outcome is predictable, as Verrier Elwin describes *"detribalization favours a few gifted individuals who are able to assimilate the new way of life, it generally deprives the mass of the people of their standards and values without replacing it with anything comparable"*.[4]

Response of Independent India

Recognizing the distinct situation and requirements of the tribal communities, the Constitution of India in the Fifth Schedule made provisions for protection of the scheduled tribes from alienation of their lands and natural resources. Independent India thus had the opportunity to undo all the historical injustices, perhaps it was on this note that Pt. Jawaharlal Nehru, the first Prime Minister of Independent India, promoted the *Panchsheel* for tribal development, *'steering clear of the excesses of both 'isolationism' and the implied civilisational arrogance of `assimilation"*. The basic tenets of this governing principle are as follows:

- Tribals should develop along the lines of their own genius and we would avoid imposing anything on them. We should try to encourage in every way their own traditional arts and culture.

- Tribal rights in land and forest should be respected.

- We should try to train and build up a team of their own people to do the work of administration and development. Some technical

---

[4] Elwin, A Philosophy of NEFA, 4

personnel from outside will, no doubt, be needed, especially in the beginning. But we should avoid introducing too many outsiders into tribal territory.

•   We should not over-administer these areas or overwhelm them with a multiplicity of schemes. We should rather work through, and not in rivalry to, their own social and cultural institutions.

•   We should judge results, not by statistics or amount of money spent, but by quality of human character that is evolved. [5]

Unfortunately these principles remained on paper and in thoughts and were also impossible for non-tribal administrators to implement. Panchsheel principles were aimed at giving protection so that no outsider could take possession of tribal land or forests or interfere with them in any way except with their consent. It was Nehru's desire that the high sense of discipline, power to enjoy life and the love for dance and song will endure among tribals. "*I am anxious that they should advance, but more anxious that they should not lose their artistry and joy that distinguishes them. Development must be according to their own genius and not something that they cannot absorb or imbibe and which merely uproots them*".[6]

The Post Independence Colonial Hangover

Subsequently, independent India's desire for a fast growth and to be counted amongst the developed nations ushered in a series of forest related laws that instead of enabling a peaceful co-existence of the tribals with the forest, pushed them out of their natural habitat leaving them restricted access to the forest and their produce. In fact, Independent Indian authority (the burra sahibs) almost replaced the colonial rulers. The *Imperial Forest Department of 1864* is not too distant a cousin of the various Forest Departments in the country identifying its primary function as that of protection, conservation and regeneration of forests with scant regard to the symbiotic people-forest

---

[5] Rann Singh Mann, Culture and Integration of Indian Tribes, (New Delhi: MD Publications, Ragini Gupta, 1993), 36

[6] Ibid., 41

relation, continues to govern their attitude. The *Indian Forest Act of 1927* upheld as the most prominent tool even today, since colonial times, enables to declare all lands not claimed by private individuals and agencies as forest lands classifying them into reserve, protected and village forests. A mere notification by Forest Department can constitute any forest land or waste land as reserved forest thereby penalizing generation long inhabitants of the forests as encroachers.

About 4.5% of the total land in the country is declared protected area, classified into national parks, wildlife sanctuaries and protected areas. *The Wildlife (Protection) Act of 1972* provided for the administration of these areas places several restrictions on the residents of villages in these areas. The *Forest Resolution Policy of 1952* reasserted colonial notions of forest management with the help of external administrators, reorienting the colonial policy to accommodate demands of the industry for raw material. Revised further in 1988, *the National Forest Policy* focused on conservation and meeting subsistence requirements of local communities rather than earning revenue. The *Forest Conservation Act of 1980* restricted use of forest land for non-forest purpose. Under both the Wildlife Protection Act and Forest Conservation Act, clearing of forest patches for cultivation or hunting of animals and birds for domestic consumption was banned. Absence of alternate effective nutritional supplement had a telling impact on the health of the tribals. *The Biodiversity Act of 2002* restricted use of herbal medicines for indigenous treatment by tribal mendicants. In absence of an alternate effective public health system, the tribals along with other non-tribal poor communities continue to suffer chronic illnesses. Finally after a long drawn debate between conservationists and tribal rights activists, the enactment of The Scheduled Tribes and Other Traditional Forest Dwellers (Recognition of Forest Rights) Act of 2006 promises to undo the historical injustices.

Towards Inclusive Growth

It would be perhaps unfair to state that the modern Indian State fully ignored the tribal communities. Due to public pressures from civil society organizations, activists, enlightened and senior citizens and bureaucrats some very vital and path-breaking measures were taken to turn the clock around. However, were they sincerely implemented? Did the 63 year-old Independent India show the political will to ensure the tribal communities their much needed social justice? Some of these progressive sets of protective laws and laws related to social justice and the mockery of these are discussed below:

Protective Laws against Land Alienation

In accordance with the Constitutional provisions in Scheduled V areas (whereby the rights of scheduled tribes over land and forests are justifiable) a series of legislations were enacted by the concerned state governments. These legislations strictly prohibited transfer of land from tribals to non-tribals recognizing the fact that non-tribals have the skill of taking advantage of the simplicity of tribals. It also recognizes that land, especially the kind of land that the tribal community resides in and works on, is central to their existence therefore calling for protection. Despite these provisions, the alienation of tribals from their land has been phenomenal.[7] Not only have non-tribals tricked the legislations through fraudulent means in dispossessing tribals of their land in complicity with the bureaucracy, but many state governments, such as Orissa and Andhra Pradesh have actively sought to amend these legislations to enable the corporate to acquire land.

Ministry of Rural Development in its annual report (2007-08) for the first time took a statewise stock of the alienation and restoration of tribal land.[8] It is pertinent to note that out of the nine Schedule V states, seven are said to be Left Wing Extremist Affected. All these states have stringent legislations to disallow transfer of land from tribal to non-tribals and further with requisite amendments to the Act enabled restoration of land back to the tribals. Yet, despite these measures, a large number of tribal families seem to have been dispossessed of their land.

---

[7] Ministry of Rural Development, "Report of the Committee on State Agrarian Relations and the Unfinished Tasks of Land Reform, (New Delhi: Government of India, 2009), http://www.rd.ap.gov.in/IKPLand/MRD_Committee_Report_V_01_Mar_09.pdf , Accessed on 13 December 2010.

[8] Department of Land Records, Ministry of Rural Development, "Annexure xviii", Annual Report 2007-08, State-wise Information on Alienation and Restoration of Tribal Lands, New Delhi, Government of India , 2007-2008

In Andhra Pradesh, for instance, *Andhra Pradesh Scheduled Areas Land Transfer Regulation, 1959* (further amended by Regulation 1 of 1970) is stringent in not only disallowing sale of land from tribal to non-tribals, but with the amendment (Regulation 1) in 1970, all non-tribals in possession of land in the scheduled districts had to prove their legal possession. But despite such measures out of the 65,875 cases filed in the Court, only 26,475 cases were decided in favour of the tribals; *The Orissa Scheduled Areas Transfer of Immovable Property (by Scheduled Tribe) Regulation 1956* has been in existence for more than half a century, and does, as already mentioned, enjoy the double protection of Schedule-5 and Schedule-9 of the Constitution. Besides the *Sections 22 and 23 of Orissa Land Revenue Act (OLRA) 1960* provide for prohibition of transfer of land from an ST to a non-ST person or from an SC to a non-SC person respectively. Of the total 105,491 cases filed in Court, only 61,431 cases were decided in favour of tribal's. This is more than indicative of the nexus of tribal land grabbers and bureaucrats to scuttle the avowed intentions of the law. In fact, Regulation-2 has provisions for bureaucrats such as Collector/Sub-Collector in the guise of Competent Authority and in OLRA the concerned Revenue Officer have been given discretionary powers using which they have been legitimizing the alienation of tribal and Dalit land. Further, *Orissa Prevention of Land Encroachment Act, 1972 and Rules 1985* were aimed at prohibiting unauthorized encroachment of government land, and in certain cases settlement of encroached land in favour of the concerned occupiers. Madhya Pradesh, on the other hand, decided not a single case in favour of tribals of the total 53,806 cases filed in the Court. This despite its progressive *Madhya Pradesh Land Revenue Code, 1959* and significant amendments of 1976 and 1980 particularly through Section 170 (B), whereby it instituted *suo moto* responsibility of the revenue court to enquire into all transactions from tribal to non-tribal, even without an application from the tribal. The burden of proof was shifted to the non-tribal to prove that fraud did not take place, and the presumption of the court supported the legal rights of the original tribal landowner. Appearance of advocates without permission has also been debarred in these proceedings. There is provision for a single appeal to the Collector. In addition, Madhya Pradesh was also the only state to make appropriate amendments in their State Laws

/ Acts which impinge on specific provisions contained in the Central Act namely (i) Land Acquisition Act; (ii) Excise Act; (iii) State Irrigation Act; (iv) Minor Forest Produce Act; (v) Mines and Minerals Acts; (vi) Land Revenue Code / Act; (vii) SC/ST Land Alienation Act; (viii) Money Lenders Act; and (ix) Regulated Market Act. No doubt, some State Governments (MP) have already amended some of the relevant Acts, others are yet to follow suit. But working in these areas one notices the blatant advantage of the entrusted discretionary powers abused by Sub-Collectors, Tahsildars and Revenue Inspector, in conniving with the vested interests to encroach more and more Government land, by way of harassing the tribal and Dalit families by way of instituting false cases against them, extorting bribes from them and distributed Patta on the encroached land to ineligible persons out of extraneous considerations.

Table No. 1

State-wise Information on Alienation and Restoration of Tribal Lands

State	No. of cases filed in court	Area	Cases disposed by the court	Area	Cases Rejected	Area	Cases Pending in Court	Area	Cases decided in favour of tribals	Area	Cases in which Land restored to tribals	Area
Andhra Pradesh	65875	287776	58212	256452	31737	150227	7663	31324	26475	106225	23383	94312
Chhattisgarh	47304	NR	46807	NR	NR	NR	79	4192	21348	43803	21269	43620
Jharkhand	5382	4002	1362	NA	283	NA	4020	NA	1079	860	1079	860
Madhya Pradesh	53806	158398	29596	97123	29596	97123	24210	61275	NR	NR	NR	NR
Maharashtra	45634	NR	44624	99486	24681	NR	1010	NR	19943	99486	19943	99486
Orissa	105491	104742	104644	103556	43213	46677	847	1186	61431	56879	61364	56854

Source: Ministry of Rural Development, Annual Report 2007-08, Annexure xvii

The Provisions of the Panchayats (Extension to the Scheduled Areas) Act, 1996 (PESA)

Soon after the 73rd and 74th Amendment of the Constitution to make way for village level decentralized governance system in 1993, pressures were built by organizations such as Bharat Jan Andolan to look at the situation of the tribal communities separately. This resulted in constituting the Bhuria Committee led by Dilip Singh Bhuria, a former Member of Parliament, to extend the provisions of part IX of the Constitution concerning panchayats to the scheduled areas.[9]

Through this bill the gram sabha was empowered to prevent alienation of land or restore land alienated, in scheduled areas, exercise control over money lending, plan development activities as per their requirements and issue utilization certificates for work undertaken in their villages, recommend grant of lease for mining activities, enjoy the right to be consulted on matters of land acquisition, etc.

When passed in 1996, the central PESA envisaged that the nine states within Schedule Five areas would enact their own legislations devolving power to their respective tribal communities, as well as amend pre-existing laws to bring them in harmony with PESA within a year. Soon after the 'naxal threat' became too difficult to handle, concerned Ministries began taking stock of the implementation of the policies within their jurisdiction to keep their units spotless. One such study commissioned by the Ministry of Panchayati Raj on the status of implementation of PESA particularly in Left-wing Extremist states revealed that '*contrary legal and administrative subterfuge has kept the provisions of PESA as a set of aspirations and the agenda of self governance remains postponed.*'[10] The academic review

---

[9] Schedule V areas include the states of Andhra Pradesh, Jharkhand, Gujarat, Himachal Pradesh, Madhya Pradesh, Chhattisgarh, Maharashtra, Orissa and Rajasthan; Schedule VI areas include the states of Assam, Meghalaya, Tripura and Mizoram.

[10] Ajay Dandekar and Chitragada Choudhuri, PESA, Left-Wing Extremism and Governance: Concerns and Challenges in India's Tribal Districts, Institute of Rural Management, Anand; Commissioned by Ministry of Panchayati Raj, Government of India, 2010, http://www.tehelka.com/channels/News/2010/july/10/PESAchapter.pdf Accessed on 5 August 2010.

exposes not just tardy implementation of PESA but even disregard of the Act, weak role of the Governors of States who have been vested with exclusive powers by the Act, sale of land from tribals to non-tribals in Schedule V areas, further in complete disregard to PESA acquisition of land continues alienating tribals despite protection laws. The review study brought out that other than Madhya Pradesh and Chhattisgarh, none of the other states appear to have made the required legislative provisions for conducive empowerment of the gram sabha. Though, ironically despite these provisions, both Madhya Pradesh and Chhattisgarh account for high numbers of cases of violations of PESA. For instance,

> "They asked us to hold a Gram Sabhas and there was police everywhere.' said one of the village-leaders of Sirisguda, in a meeting with the Express a few days ago, 'And yet we said no to Tata!'... reports on the nature of public hearing held by Tatas to set up a steel factory in Lohandiguda, Bastar district, Chhattisgarh.... a public hearing held on the 5th of May, 2010 in Dantewada district, regarding the NMDC in Kirandul, was considered fraudulent as many of the villages who'd be directly affected by the project weren't even present during the hearing. 'The public hearing was held 50 kilometres away from the affected villages, and the people at the hearing were contractors and other lackeys of the NMDC ..."[11]

The Scheduled Tribes and Other Traditional Forest Dwellers (Recognition of Forest Rights) Act, 2006 (or the Forest Rights Act)

The Forest Rights Act is lauded as one of the progressive steps in correcting historical injustice meted to tribal communities for generations, all set to provide for the restitution of deprived forest rights across India, including both individual rights to cultivated land in forested landscapes and collective rights to control manage and use forests as common property.

---

[11] Javed Iqbal, The New Indian Express, 22 August, 2010

The Act covers two key aspects:

- Private and/or communal land ownership rights, including restitution for past illegal eviction / displacement.

- Community resource use rights, including collective management of common (or community) forest resources; rights over common property resources such as produce of water bodies; grazing rights (both for settled and nomadic communities); rights over 'habitat' for 'Primitive Tribal Groups'; other customary rights and usufruct (actually 'ownership') rights over Non Timber Forest Produce (although there is someambiguity over whether these shall be community' or individual rights).

Thus the Act is not just a forest land rights act, but that which recognizes rights over forest resources. If interpreted and implemented in all sincerity it has more than strong chances of restoring dignity to the forest dependent communities and recognizing them as one of the key decision makers in the growth of the country.

The Ministry of Tribal Affairs in its status report on the implementation of the FRA until 30th September 2010 records that 34.72% of titles have been distributed over number of claims received while 64.24 per cent have been rejected. This status report is of 27 states; 12 states have not made any distribution of land entitlements against the said act so far. Of the claims received and accepted (in spite of and after over 50% rejections!), some of the states have done impressive distribution, such as Chhattisgarh (98.98%), Andhra Pradesh (95.99%), Karnataka (88.03%), Madhya Pradesh (87.18%) but these very states have also rejected more than 50% of the claims; Chhattisgarh (55.24%); Andhra Pradesh (45.44%); Karnataka (84.81%, Madhya Pradesh (63.0%).

A joint review to assess the implementation of the Forest Rights Act was conducted by the Ministry of Tribal Affairs and Ministry of Environment and Forests recently undertook visits to 9 states in July-August 2010 under the chairmanship of Shri N C Saxena which once again reveals utter lack of commitment of the governments in empowering its tribal populace, almost edging on a deliberate attempt to keep them impoverished and disempowered. The full report is yet to be released, but a note by Mr Saxena on the visit to Chhattisgarh that claims 98.99% of distribution of 'rightful' claims, reveals some disturbing facts.[12] The same is mentioned below.

Implementation of Forest Rights Act in Chhattisgarh, N C Saxena, visit report of May 2010

a. Most of the rejections of applications have been hastily made based on the report by patwaris or forest guard without any verification, the decisions of the rejections were not made known to applicants thereby leaving them in a limbo, unable to exercise the right to appeal there have been blanket rejections of applications from areas under National Parks, especially in Bastar region;

b. when granted area mentioned in the title was far less than the area occupied – this error was due to unclear information with the villagers who left the column blank;

c. Particularly vulnerable Tribal Groups (PTGs) and nomadic tribes were not given priority as required under Rule 8(b);

d. although the Act requires titles to be given in joint names of both the spouses, wives names were left out in most cases;

e. roles played by the Department for Tribal Development, the nodal agency to roll out the FRA and the State Level Monitoring Committee have been abysmally poor in providing the enabling environment for the forest dependent communities to get justice.

Scheduled Castes and Scheduled Tribes (Prevention of Atrocities) Act, 1989

The SC & ST (PoA) Act 1989 is the only Act which aims to eliminate atrocities that are occurring against members of the SCs and STs while at the same time providing protection, compensation and rehabilitation to victims.

As per National Crime Records Bureau (NCRB) 2008 report, 1,022

---

[12] N.C. Saxena, " Implementation of Forest Rights Act in Chhattisgarh: report of Field Visit, 24-27 July 2010", MoEF/ MoTA Committee on Forest Rights Act, Government of India, 2010,http://www.fra.org.in/Chhattisgarh%20visit%20note,%20NC%20Saxena% 20_FINAL_.pdf, Accessed on August 5, 2010.

cases have been registered against STs under the SC/ST Act. The average conviction rate for crimes against Scheduled tribes is recorded as 27.2% as compared to overall conviction rate of 42.6% relating to IPC cases and 83.5% relating to SLL cases (such as Protection of Civil Liberties Act and SC/ST Prevention of Atrocities Act).

The extent of crime against scheduled tribes in the so-called Left-Wing Extremist States is coincidentally very high, in fact most of these states are ranked high (*see Table below*) according to percentage share to an all India crime.

Table 2: Incidence of Crime Against ST's in LWE States

States	Incidences	Percentage contribution to all India	Rank as per percentage share
Total	5582	100	
Madhya Pradesh	1071	19.2	1
Andhra Pradesh	750	13.4	3
Chhattisgarh	614	11.0	4
Orissa	508	9.1	5
Maharashtra	268	4.8	7
Jharkhand	231	4.1	8
West Bengal	17	0.3	14

Source: NCBR, 2008

Bonded Labour System (Abolition) Act, 1976

The bonded labour system was abolished by law throughout the country w.e.f 25th October 1975 by an Ordinance following India's ratification of ILO Convention No.29 (Forced Labour Convention 1930) on 30.11.1954. The Bonded Labour System (Abolition) Act was passed by the Parliament in 1976. The Act provides for the abolition of bonded labour, bonded labour system and bonded debt. In a survey conducted by National Human Rights Commission (NHRC) in October-December 1996, the behest of the Supreme Court of India, the report identified the problem of bonded labour to be 'closely linked to the broader socio-economic problems of limited economic opportunities, landlessness, irregular and low wages, poor conditions of agricultural land, inherently faulty policies and land reforms, caste based discrimination/ social exclusion, illiteracy, exploitative share cropping system, cultural and religious belief and historical legacy. The survey identified high incidence of bonded labour in the agriculture sector in the States of Andhra Pradesh, Bihar, Haryana, Karnataka, Maharashtra, Orissa, Punjab, Tamilnadu and Madhya Pradesh and an aggravated form of deprivation and exploitation in the form of migrant bonded labour in the States of Bihar, Jharkhand, Chattisgarh, Tamilnadu, Madhya Pradesh, Orissa, Rajasthan. As per estimate of the Programme Evaluation Organization of the Planning Commission, 83.2% of the total number of bonded labourers belonged to SCs and STs (Special Report of National Commission for SCs said STs)

The 1996 Survey conducted by the Ministry of Labour records 2,85,379 persons as 'identified and released' until 31st March 2004. According to the survey, the Scheduled Tribes were bonded as plantation workers (Malekudiya tribals of Karnataka),as agricultural labourers (Koya tribes of Malkangiri, Orissa), as unskilled stone quarry workers (Kol tribes of Uttar Pradesh) in silica and sandstone mining of Shankargarh, Allahabad (Sahariya tribes of Uttar Pradesh), as food gatherers of Sago Palm (Sullong tribes of Arunachal Pradesh);as brick kiln workers (Scheduled Castes and Tribes from Madhya Pradesh, Chhattisgarh, Andhra Pradesh, Gujarat, Orissa, etc.), as weavers in power looms (from Tamil Nadu), as construction workers (Andhra Pradesh, Madhya Pradesh

The Working Paper series Special Action Programme to combat Forced Labour by ILO, Geneva, April 2005 notes that S*cheduled Tribes belonging to Orissa, Chhattisgarh, Haryana, Madhya Pradesh, Southern Uttar Pradesh, Uttaranchal, Andhra Pradesh, Maharashtra, Rajasthan and Gujarat, who* *have suffered a gradual erosion of access to traditional livelihood systems, have long been subject to exploitative debt relations leading to loss of land and bondage to non-tribals[13].*

Child Labour (Prohibition and Regulation) Act, 1986

The curbing of child bonded servitude was attempted before independence by the British government with the enactment of Children (Pledging of Labour) Act of 1933. However, despite the Act, the practice continued and got aggravated calling for the Child Labour (Prohibition and Regulation) Act, 1986 that only added the list of sites of child labour with little impact on the prohibition.

Human Rights Watch (1996), based on a survey of 100 bonded children in five states (Rajasthan, Tamil Nadu, Karnataka, Maharashtra and Uttar Pradesh), has identified bonded child labour in a number of occupations including agriculture, brick kilns, stone quarries, carpet weaving, bidi rolling, rearing of silk cocoons, production of silk saris, silver jewellery, synthetic gemstones, precious gem cutting, diamond cutting, leather products etc. These children are made to work against debt taken by their parents or guardians, at low or no wages, from a very young age.

A report published by NHRC[14] observes that States having a larger population living below the poverty line have a higher incidence of child labour. Consequently, higher incidence of child labour is accompanied by high dropout rates in schools. A logical extension of this observation is to co-relate the percent of BPL families amongst Scheduled Tribes to the states with high prevalence of child labour. This would point to high incidence of prevalence of child labour amongst Scheduled Tribes. (though one must make a note that Orissa surprisingly falls out of this argument)

---

[13] Ravi Srivastava, " Bonded Labour in India: Its Incidence and Pattern", Forced Labour, Paper No. 18, InFocus Programme on Promoting the Declaration on Fundamental Principles and Rights at Work and International Labour Office, April 2005, http://digitalcommons.ilr.cornell.edu/forcedlabor/18/, Accessed 5 September 2010.

[14] National Human Rights Commission, " Know Your Rights- Child Labour", Government of India, 2004-05, http://www.nhrc.nic.in/Publications/KnowYourRights.pdf, Accessed 5 September 2010.

Table 3: Extent of Child Labour in India

States	Percentage
Andhra Pradesh	14.5
Uttar Pradesh	12.5
Madhya Pradesh	12.0
Karnataka	8.7
Maharashtra	9.5
Bihar	8.3
Rajasthan	6.9
West Bengal	6.3
Tamil Nadu	5.1
Gujarat	4.6
Orissa	4.0

Source: National Human Rights Commission, " Know Your Rights- Child Labour", Government of India, 2004-05, http://www.nhrc.nic.in/Publications/ KnowYourRights.pdf, Accessed 5 September 2010

Inter-State Migrant Workmen (Regulation of Employment and Conditions of Services) Act, 1979

Recognizing high levels of inter-state migration for labour, this Act was enacted to check exploitation. As per the census of the year 1991, nearly 20 million people migrated to other states seeking livelihood. Within a decade, the number of interstate migration doubled to 41,166,265 persons as per the census figures of 2001. It is estimated that, the present strength of inter state migrants is around 80 million persons of which, 40 million are in the construction industry, 20 million as domestic workers, 2 million as sex workers, 5 million as call girls and from half a million to 12 million in the illegal mines otherwise called as "small scale mines"[15].

Circular migration or rural-urban migration rates are high in remote rural areas, particularly amongst chronically poor people. Particularly high rates are found in drought prone areas with low agro-ecological potential, poor access to credit or other pre-requisites for diversification and high population densities. Studies undertaken in Madhya Pradesh, Andhra Pradesh and Orissa reveal that circular migration is particularly high among the poor, scheduled castes (SCs), scheduled tribes (STs) and Muslims. Further, the report shares that short-term migration is higher among poorer groups, involving over 80% of the landless and 88% of illiterate people and migration among SCs and STs is nearly twice that of the upper castes (15% of the SC/ST households compared to 8% of upper caste households).[16] Permanent migration rates are higher among the more educated but illiterate and unskilled people appear to dominate seasonal labour migration.[17] This Act however, remains only a piece of paper as most States do not cooperate and tend to protect the interest of the employers.

Impact on Tribal Communities

High Instance of Poverty amongst Scheduled Tribes

The percentage of families living below poverty line (BPL), both rural and urban combined is estimated at 27.5 in 2004 of which an estimated 15 per cent belong to Scheduled Tribes. Of this 47.3% of BPL STs live in rural areas and 33.3% live in urban areas.

A quick look at the statistics of BPL families belonging to Scheduled Tribes

---

[15] Sudarshan Rao Sarde, "Migration in India: Trade Union Perspective in the Context of Neo-Liberal Globalization", http://www.imfmetal.org/files/08102914241866/Migrant_workers_in_India.pdf, Accessed on 5 September 2010.

[16] H. Dayal and A. K. Karan, "Labour Migration from Jharkhand", (New Delhi: Institute for Human Development, 2003)

[17] Priya Deshingkar, D.Start and J. Farrington, "Changing Livelihood Contexts in the Study Locations" in J. Farrington, P. Deshingkar, C. Johnson and D Start Policy Windows and Livelihoods Future, (New Delhi: Oxford University Press, 2006)

from the states affected by Left-wing Extremist reveals a high percent of poor tribals in these states.

Nutritional status among tribal women and children

Though the overall situation of women and children in India is poor, that of tribal women and children abysmally poor.

Table 4: Percent of Population (social group wise) Below Poverty Line – 2004-05 in LWE states

States	Rural			Urban		
	ST	SC	OBC	ST	SC	OBC
All India	47.2	36.8	26.7	33.3	39.9	31.4
Madhya Pradesh	58.6	42.8	29.6	44.4	67.3	55.5
Chhattisgarh	54.7	32.7	33.9	41.0	52.0	52.7
Andhra Pradesh	30.5	15.4	9.5	50.0	39.9	28.9
Jharkhand	54.2	57.9	40.2	45.1	47.2	19.1
Orissa	75.6	50.2	36.9	61.8	72.6	50.2
Maharashtra	56.6	44.8	23.9	40.4	43.2	35.6
West Bengal	42.4	29.2	18.3	25.7	28.5	10.4

Source: 11th Five Year Plan, Vol III, Annexure 4.4, Planning Commission

Table 5: Nutritional Parameters among Tribals and Non-Tribals

Parameters	Scheduled tribes %	General population %
Malnutrition in children	54.5	33.7
Aneamia in children	76.8	70
Anaemia in women	68.5	51.3
Underweight among women	46.6	29.4
Vitamin A deficiency	30	18.5
Chronic energy deficiency	47	35

Source: Bala and Thiruselvakumar, "Overcoming Tribal Health Problems", *Indian Journal of Community Medicine*, Vol 34 (4) (October 2009)

Diseases/Ailments amongst Tribals[16]

Under conditions of extremely poor nutrition both among children and adults, the extent to which tribal communities suffer illnesses is not a surprise. The most common diseases seen among tribals are respiratory tract infections and diarrheal disorders. 21% of children suffer at least two bouts of diarrhoea every year and 22% suffer from at least two attacks of respiratory infections. Tribals account for 25% of all malaria cases occurring in India and 15% of all falciparum cases. Intestinal helminthiasis is widely prevalent among tribal children (up to 50% in Orissa and 75% in MP). Skin infections such as tinea and scabies are seen among tribals due to poor personal hygiene. Sexually transmitted diseases are relatively more common (7.2% prevalence of syphilis among Kolli hills tribals of Tamil Nadu). The prevalence of tuberculosis is high, especially in Orissa.

---

[16] Bala and Thiruselvakumar, "Overcoming Tribal Health Problems", Indian Journal of Community Medicine, Vol. 34 (4): (October 2009)

Sickle cell trait prevalence varies from 0.5% to 45%, disease prevalence is around 10%. It is mostly seen among the tribals of central and southern India, not reported in North-East. The prevalence of tobacco use is 44.9% among tribal men and 24% among tribal women.

Mortality Rate among Tribal Children

Scheduled Tribes make up 8 to 9 percent of the population, but account for about 14 percent of all under-five deaths, and 23 percent of deaths in the 1-4 age group in rural areas. Since the majority of deaths among tribal children are concentrated in the 1-4 age group (see Figure 1), in this age group, tribal deaths account for almost - a quarter of all deaths.

Table 6: High Rate of Child Mortality among Tribal Communities

Social groups	Percent of child deaths (1-5 years)-rural	Percent of Under-five deaths
SC	28.1	24.6
ST	23.0	13.9
OBC	35.5	39.6
Gen	13.4	21.9

Source: NFHS, 2005 quoted in Maitreyi B. Das, Soumya Kapoor and Denis Nikitin, "A Closer Look at Child Mortality Among Adhivasis in India", Policy Research Working Paper 5231, World Bank, South Asia Region, March 2010, URL: http:// indigenouspeoplesissues.com/attachments/4351_Adivasi_ChildMortality2010.pdf, Accessed on 23 March 2011

Growing Discontent

It should surprise any person with logic that a particular social group, such as the tribal communities, would have patiently borne such long years of injustice meted out to them in the name of development with construction of dams, roads and factories or safeguarding environment and wild life with the declaration of national parks and wild life sanctuaries or enhancing GDP through mining.

In a situation where there is a systemic effort to uproot a community that has for generations safeguarded forests and wildlife seeking nothing in return, where there is complete failure of governance with no space for redressal, is it surprising that the tribals have decided to resist any further moves to annihilate their core existence that is connected with 'Jal, Jangal and Jameen' (water, forest and land)?

Forced Displacement of Tribals

The tribals never really enjoyed the fruits of independent India, the protective laws never did insulate them from exploitation, nor did laws related to social justice offer them the necessary redressal leave alone justice. Instead they were subject to forced displacement in the name of progress and development of the country at whose altar they sacrificed their homes, tradition, culture, festivals and the very ethos of life. In fact, since Independence, India, with the blessing of our first Prime Minister, Pt Jawaharlal Nehru, raced towards 'development' of modern India with construction of large dams and massive steel plants. The subsequent prime movers of the country pursued the 'shining' India and India with a 'double-digit' growth far more aggressively giving scant consideration to the impact of these on various social groups, especially scheduled castes, scheduled tribes, women, minority communities, etc.

In a report titled Resource Rich Tribal Poor jointly published by Action Aid India, Indian Social Institute and Laya, Prof Xaxa recounts in his introductory chapter that from 1951 to 1990 an estimated 21 million people have been displaced by development projects such as dams, mines, industries and wildlife sanctuaries – over 16 million displaced by dams, 2.6 million by mines and 1.3 million by industries and a little over 1 million by other projects including wild-life sanctuaries. 40 per cent of this displaced population is tribal; in other words 8.54 million tribal people have been displaced in modern India between 1954 and 1990. A large per cent of those displaced (75%) are tribals, 52 percent of those displaced from mines and 38% of those displaced from dams. Some tribal families have faced multiple displacements.

Naxal Influence in Tribal Dominated Areas

Since mid- 2000, naxalism or Maoism, as it is interchangeably addressed, has been on the centre-stage of heated debates and discussions –regionally, nationally and globally. Even the middle class, especially the urban middle-class that keeps itself out of such ideology ridden conversations, has been drawn into expressing its opinion. In this debate, the Ruling merges with the Opposition and vice-a-versa; Centre and State even if from opposing political parties, stand united in analyzing and taking recourse to the current situation. The Government of India has estimated that the movement is now active in about 125 districts spread over 12 states[17]. 99 per cent of these are tribal dominated areas located in the states of West Bengal, Orissa, Chhattisgarh, Jharkhand, Madhya Pradesh, Maharashtra and Andhra Pradesh – which have been declared as "States affected by Left Wing Extremism". Is it then coincidental that it is in the tribal dominated blocks that Maoists are so popular? Is it also coincidental that both the State and the Centre are finding it difficult to 'contain' the Maoist influence as more and more of the tribal populace is getting increasingly influenced by them. As K Balagopalan writes '.....*the fact is that in much of this area the first time the common people experienced anything resembling justice was when the Naxalite movement spread there and taught people not to take injustice lying down...*'[18] The Naxalites or Maoists apparently performed the tasks that the elected government should have done in upholding what the Constitution provided for, such as abolition of 'begar' or payment of minimum wages. What started as the Naxalite movement in the yesteryears of the 60s and 70s against feudal domination and economic repression of the poor, posits quite differently today. With Corporates replacing the feudal landlords in wielding sufficient power over elected representatives of the people in acquiring land, ensuring eviction in complicity with state machinery such as the police, plundering the land without any compensation for the people whose homes, agricultural land and cattle are destroyed, flouting rules and

---

[17] Planning Commission, " Development Challenges in Extremist Affected Areas", Report of an Expert Group to Planning Commission, Government of India, 2008.

[18] K. Balagopal, "Physiognomy of Violence", Economic and Political Weekly, Vol. XLI, (June 3, 2006), 2183-2186.

regulations formulated to safeguard the interest of specific communities, pressing for favourable policy changes to 'enable' their 'crime' in the name of development and progress...... all this and more leaving the tribals further alienated, impoverished, helpless and now even criminalized for having taken the support of the band of people who speak their language, understand their hapless situation and appear to have promised a 'thus far, no further ...' kind of situation.

The State Responds with Security over Justice

Whether the proponents of Maoism found 'fertile ground' to lay out their blue print for acquiring 'state power' or did the tribals willingly welcomed the ideology to overcome the generation long injustice, will continue to be debated. Definitely the situation is grim as life for a peace loving community that was closest to none other than nature, stand destroyed, plundered and devastated today. The growing influence of 'naxalism' or 'Maoism' has been recognized repeatedly as the 'greatest internal security threat'. In a foolish panic of losing state power, instead of addressing generations of injustice to the tribal community, the government initially supported formation of people's vigilantes (such as the infamous Salwa Judum in Chhattisgarh) and when that failed it moved forces into the forests under the guise of Operation Green Hunt. The response thus has been the classical British response to tribal rebellions and Independence movements. Instead of looking into the conflict and understanding what the tribal rebels were stating through their resistance, the State preferred to use force to show who holds the might. Instead of addressing the tribal discontent it has preferred to use guns for conflict resolution.

The State thus exhibited a three-pronged approach to the 'naxal threat' - **first**, creating civil defense movements/committees[19] and arming

---

[19] Be it the Salwa Judum in Dantewada (Chhattisgarh) or Shanti Committee in Koraput (Orissa) or Gana Pratirodh Committee in Lalgarh (West Bengal), the State has actively created these vigilante groups to take on the task of counter-mobilization through force and information gathering in the name of seeking peace against Maoist violence. It is sad to note that people were pitted against people in this exercise building mistrust and fear of one another. Although, the initial success of these vigilante groups in subjugating the tribal way of life gave much fillip to the practice of using armed or violent civil defense

them[20](Government of Chhattisgarh inducted young boys and girls as Special Police Officers (SPOs) legally providing them with the requisite arms); **second**, greater militarization and weaponization of the police (Ministry of Home established Unified Commands for Jharkhand, Chhattisgarh, Orissa and West Bengal in September 2010 and set aside a budget of 724 crores to equip the police force in these states); ironically this also included a budget of Rs.107.19 crore for acquisition of land for the Sashastra Seema Bal (Rs.93.46 crore); Indo-Tibetan Border Police (Rs.7.04 crore) and the Border Security Force (Rs.6.69 crore). Sanctions amounting to Rs.43.23 crore were issued for the construction of residential accommodation for the Assam Rifles (Rs.28.84 crore) and the Central Reserve Police Force (CoBRA) (Rs.14.39 crore) and **thirdly** continue to sell mineral-based industrialization in tribal areas (Since the adoption of the Chhattisgarh State Mineral Policy, 2001, the government has concluded deals with several steel and power companies to establish plants in Chhattisgarh by 2010, resulting in a total investment of Rs. 182486.09 crores. These include a MoU signed with Tata Steel in June 2005 for a five million tonnes per annum (MTPA) plant in Bastar district's Lohandiguda block with an investment of Rs.100 billion, and the Essar Steel MoU in the same month for a 3.2 MTPA plant in Dhurli and Bhansi villages of Dantewada district with an investment of Rs.70 billion). Coincidentally 2005 was the year when Salwa Judum came into existence. It is relevant to note that all these approaches have only exacerbated the violence.

Where are the Tribal Concerns?

In her book *Subalterns and Sovereigns*, Nandini Sundar analyses that most of the discourse on Maoism in India is akin to 'moral panic':

"What is then at stake is the Government's image of being firm and taking action; action which may have no direct relevance or efficiency

---

groups but eventually discontent began setting in when vigilante groups began mobilizing for better facilities. (observation by the authors after extensive visits to camps, villages, spending time with the villagers, engaging in development work in the last three years)

[20] "Death, Displacement and Deprivation The War in Dantewara", A Report of the Human Rights Forum, Publication No. 14, 2006.

in tackling the problem at hand. While Maoism may not be merely a law and order problem, the reaction to it upholds a certain order, often at the expense of fundamental rights"[21]

Though force has been the main focus of State response to Maoists, it is over the last couple of years that there has been a shift from sporadic counter-insurgency to a tactical planned long-term campaign.

It becomes clear that perceptions of threat and security define the Naxalite problem rather than the actual direct violence itself. This is corroborated in the Government claim that "violent activities" were reported in 2005 from 509 out of a total of 12,476 police stations located in 76 districts in the country.[22] It also goes on to state that while Maoists are better armed than before and their cadres receive arms training, incidents of violence were confined to just 4 % of total police stations. In fact, activists and academia who echo Nandini Sundar's observations relate that the hyperbole of security is a camouflage of the greater need for near permanent presence of security forces to facilitate large-scale land acquisition for the billions waiting to be invested in the densely forested and mineral rich habitats of tribals hence the wrath of the Green Hunt is concentrated in highlands of central India. It is also a justification for diversion, often unaccountable for the huge funding and force multiplication of the military power of the State.

In such a context, exercises such as Operation Green Hunt "a prolonged, open-ended engagement" rather than a short, fierce "operation" grows into instances of "terrible oppression, daily firings and indiscriminate arrests of people" in the name of 'combing and search operations', 'sanitization processes', 'road security operations', 'identification of ambush prone areas', 'nabbing naxal elements' and stresses the state to divert its resources for such exercises and the villagers whose life is harassed and disrupted. Unfortunately the State in this process only ends up accumulating further accusations of human rights violations rather than addressing the real issue. In a conflict situation, principles of human rights are seldom respected, the

---

[21] Nandini Sundar, Subalterns and Sovereigns: An Anthropological History of Bastar (1854-2006), (USA: Oxford University Press, 2007).

[22] Ministry of Home Affairs, "Annual Report 2005-2006, Government of India, 2006, p- 24.

rule of law is abandoned and basic governance collapses. This leads to piled up accusations, counter-accusations, protest by civil rights groups, clamp down on civil rights groups, cases of illegal detentions, overflowing prisons, cases against civil rights activists, encounter killings, cover-ups for fake encounters, press-conferences, charges, counter charges, accusations and counteraccusations etc. The vicious cycle continues. What happens to the real issues related to tribal concerns, is anybody's guess.

Militarisation vs Development

One cursory look at the infrastructure facility in a district like Dantewada will speak volumes to the development approach adopted by the State.

Number of Police Stations	–	34
ICDS Centres	–	7
Primary Health Centres	–	24
Government Secondary schools	–	16
Government Senior Secondary Schools	–	12
Government Degree College	–	3

In August – September 2010, Bijapur district of Chhattisgarh witnessed over 200 deaths due to cholera and severe contamination of lifeline Rivers like the Talperu, Indravati and Vansadhara. The government infrastructure was deplorably inadequate to respond to this outburst. Health workers from voluntary agencies visiting the region found the roads abandoned and untraveled for many years. Government health personnel refused to enter the region under the pretext of 'naxal threat' and villagers suffered and many died as a result.

Soon after the launch of the embarrassing ambush and tragic death of 76 CRPF personnel in Dantewada, the State government with the help of the Centre began mass recruitment of tribal youth into police forces. Around 5,000 SPOs have been already appointed in Chhattisgarh and a special Koya Commandos has been established from the SPOs; there is an additional sanction by the Ministry of Home Affairs for more recruitments;

Chhattisgarh has plans to recruit an additional 3000 SPOs[23].

Deaths among tribal SPOs and local tribal policemen has increased[24] - Andhra Pradesh is raising two *'girijan'* battalions from agency areas, which would comprise people from tribal and settler communities. Orissa government is raising a tribal force of 6,000 and Jharkhand is raising *'pahari'* battalions, apart from the recruited special force of 14,000 to fight Maoists. "On April 25, 2006 Bihar announced distribution of arms licenses to "help villagers combat Maoists" as well as provide arms to five persons in each village in Aurangabad district. While Home Minister of Chhattisgarh says, "we need 50 battalions of paramilitary forces"[25], the State has been infamous for its recruitment of special police officers (SPOs) and village defense committees (VDCs)"[26]

Where does this leave the Tribals?

Where has all this militarization and 'development' left the tribals today? Dead at the crossfire; a crossfire of bullets and a gross fire of hunger in the belly. While tribal families have been condemned to a life of fear and uncertainty, as a community they have been brutally criminalized and uprooted. Branded as Maoists by the State, internal displacement and forced migration are the only survival options left to every rural family in the conflict zones. Complicated further with false cases foisted on hapless men and women, alienation from permanent sources of livelihood and mounting forest offenses from an even more hostile forest department, tribals have become fugitives in their own land.

---

[23] "Centre Approves 3000 more SPOs, More Payment", Chattisgarh Top News, 28th August 2010, http://www.chhattisgarhtopnews.com/inner.asp?aa=980, Accessed 5 September 2010.

[24] There is unfortunately no data with us to substantiate this, but conversations with local people have confirmed this. Since they are familiar with local route, they are, most often, pushed in the front to end up as casualties of bomb blasts or firings.

[25] Indian Express, 26 March 2006.

[26] Gautam Navlakha, " Maoists in India", Economic and Political Weekly, June 3, 2006, 2186-2189.

A Community Criminalized and Uprooted

Tribals in Maoist-influenced areas *(the authors cannot agree with using the word 'control' which presumes a total capture of state power over an area and we have never seen any such area.)* have been criminalized. An intentional branding of tribals living in these influence zones as Maoists has deprived an entire community the basic right to life. A fact finding exercise by the Chhattisgarh Chapter of People's Union for Civil Liberties (PUCL) has observed the following aspects of a community that has been cruelly criminalized and uprooted:

a.   Police and the administration in Andhra Pradesh have been categorical in sending across messages that *new migrants entering Andhra borders if identified will be forcibly sent back to Chhattisgarh.* This has created a wave of fear among both new and old migrants as a result these migrants even fear disclosing their identity.

b.   Salwa Judum members of Chhattisgarh have been holding meetings in village bazaars of Andhra Pradesh adjoining their State borders *threatening local residents from offering any kind of support,* shelter and protection to the new migrants.

c.   In the last one-and-half years several *'bind-over'*[27] cases have *been slapped* on the new migrants, old migrants and local Koya inhabitants. Almost all villages we visited had at least one member in the family with 'bind over' charges. There is at the moment no record on the number of 'bind over' cases in the district, but Human Rights Forum estimates it should run into hundreds. It was gathered that only men are issued these charges. Despite the fact that such

---

[27] Binding over is a precautionary measure, adopted when there is reasonable ground to anticipate present or future danger. It is not a conviction or punishment. It is not considered an alternative measure in those cases where the prosecution has insufficient evidence to substantiate a charge. Magistrates can bind over any person to good behaviour or keep the peace. This may happen where the case involves violence or threat of it. Sometimes prosecution will drop a charge if the defendant agrees to be bound over in this way. No conviction is recorded if the matter is dealt with like this because such an order is regarded as a civil matter.

bind over charges are executed by the order of the Mandal Revenue Officer who is required to first investigate evidences against the person and once convinced order the person to be 'bound over'. The current practice involves getting the person into the *thana* and have her/his thumb impression forcibly taken on a statement that ranges from offering protection or food to Maoists or actively supporting them. Bound-over people are then expected to report in the *thana* once a week narrating their whereabouts or providing information about anyone suspicious, etc. They are made to go around in an auto to gather posters or *parchas* left by the Maoists and report anything suspicious.

d. Families that have migrated to Andhra Pradesh are taken to local *thana where photographs of men, women and children are taken to keep a record*. These methods are used to "restrict influx". Random checks are later made in houses if new migrants have arrived. In one village, we were informed how a couple who had reached a week back were picked up and dropped off at the border by the police

The net result of this criminalization is that the tribals that are seen regularly at police stations are viewed with suspicion by the Maoists. If this persists then the end is death by summary execution. The Maoists on their part have failed to see the vulnerability of the 'trapped' tribals. If they do not obey the diktats of police officials it would mean false cases and jail term for 'god-knows-how-many-years'. If they do as the police say, the Maoist wrath befalls them. With neither conflict party empathizing with the forcibly displaced people, they have become a condemned and criminalized lot.

A further impact of this criminalization is that tribal families are ripped apart into two. While one brother gets into the CPI Maoist as its cadre, one joins the police as SPO and the other perhaps migrates to Andhra as an IDP. The conflict has thus torn apart families and this has in turn fragmented tribal communities which were inherently cohesive. Villages in South Chhattisgarh and South Orissa have been subject to violent assaults by the State and Maoists alike. Going either way, police or Maoist, is not a choice but a matter of survival. The criminalization, either as Maoist-hunted SPOs or SPO-hunted Maoists has killed a once culturally vibrant and economically thriving community of Koyas, Murias, Dorlas and Duruas. The State however is more worried about its pending investments and Maoists about their revolution.

Fugitives in their Own Land

Due to the branding, followed by the persecution by both the police and the Maoists there has been a large exodus of tribals fleeing Chhattisgarh in two phases, especially from Konta and Sukma blocks of Dantewada district and Bhopalpatnam block of Bijapur district. The forced migrants or IDPs have built new settlements in Bhadrachalam, Cherla, Burgampadu, Chinturu, Kothagudem, Palavancha, Venkatapuram and Wajedu Mandals (blocks) of Khammam district and Eturnagram Mandal of Warangal district. The strategy of branding and uprooting is a reminder of what American defense analysts would say "drain the water to kill the fish". Government analysis lies on the fact that when tribals remain in their villages they support the Maoists and provide food and shelter. Thus it is necessary to displace tribals from the villages in order to cut the 'supply line' to Maoists. Branding and uprooting is a convenient strategy as it turns tribals into fugitives without as much as taking the pains to counter-mobilise them.

Against this background, it is interesting to quote the District Collector of Dantewada who is categoric when he says: *"to end the problem of Naxalites it is not enough to kill Naxalites but .... to crush and destroy their system operating at the village level"*[28]

Visits by the authors into the new destination of the migrant tribals in Andhra Pradesh reveals that a different pattern in migration has emerged post 2005 i.e. since inception of Salwa Judum. Villagers from 644 villages fled to their relatively familiar place of Andhra Pradesh where they used to annually come for chilly harvesting, but post 2005 a different pattern has emerged where families refused to return to their homes in Chhattisgarh refusing to be pawns in the hands of Government via Salwa Judum activists or be associated with Maoists. They neither wanted to live in the camps,

---

[28] Ibid, 2187

as insisted by the Government, nor could they live in their villages as they desired, for fear of being caught in the cross-fire. At that point of time, organizations working in those areas quoted that nearly 50,000 persons had moved over to Andhra. However, an official survey conducted by an NGO and Integrated Tribal Development Agency (ITDA) recorded that 16,000 persons had migrated into Andhra from Chhattisgarh[29]. Based on this job cards were issued to the families and bridge schools opened after much lobbying by the civil society groups in Andhra and recommendations from NCPCR (National Commission for the Protection of Child Rights) in 2007.[30] Currently four bridge schools are running in Khammam district and more than 400 IDP children are studying in these schools. Very recently, about 111 children were admitted into the regular Ashram schools.

Post September 2010, with the launch of Operation Green Hunt, mass migration began once again and the miseries were manifold and worse. No official survey exists to record exact number of families fleeing from Chhattisgarh. An NGO survey in Khammam district in January-February 2010 recorded 352 families as the new set of IDPs post October 2009. This figure once again may not be exact as the movement of people between the borders is becoming more and more invisible, risky and fraught with danger. Movement of people into Warangal district is also reported, but no figures are currently available, nor is their situation known.

Those who reached the forests cleared patches inside the reserve forests to build settlements who had relatives in Andhra were absorbed in the settled old habitations of the natives, but the Murias did not have this advantage and hence had to create their settlements and this put them in direct conflict with the forest officials. The Murias bore the brunt of criminalization by the police because for the police 'tribals living inside reserve forests' are a potential combination for Maoist mobilization!

---

[29] IDP Joint Survey Report, ASDS and Ministry of Tribal Welfare, October 2009.

[30] Visit Report to Dantewada (Chhattisgarh) & Khammam (Andhra Pradesh) to Investigate Status of Health and Education of Children affected by Civil Unrest,17th to 19th December 2007, NCPCR.

Livelihood Sources Disrupted and Destroyed

Conflict has destroyed forest and land as stable sources of livelihood and forced migration, the only option left to tribals for survival is as wage workers with whatever wages given, migration to cities and other urban centres as low paid labourers or selling non-timber forest products and vegetables or anything they can find some buyers for. All these sources are wrought with risks to life and health, with poor remuneration and with denial of basic rights.[31] This pushes tribals into a spiral of structural violence seeking retribution through direct confrontation with state apparatus, motivated by a revolutionary ideology.

NREGS work for IDPs and people in the heart of the conflict zones is available but perhaps only on paper. During field visits it was found that most households in IDP settlements and interior conflict zone villages had NREGS job cards but not a single day of work. Even if they did get work, the waiting period for payments was as long as two years in some cases. The most intriguing fact is that NGO workers in the area have confirmed that Government officials along with the police use NREGS cards as a clandestine exercise for the identification of IDPs as well as people living in conflict zone villages. This perhaps explains the omnipresence of NREGS cards along with the missing work availability and payment delays.

Migration to unknown cities as low paid labourers is a common survival strategy among conflict-affected tribal families. Mostly it is the youth and men below 40 years who prefer this option. They travel to metros and urban centres to work with bore-well companies, in brick kilns and at construction sites for wages as low as Rs 35 a day with food costs cut from their total payable wages at the time of their leaving. Many times, the migrants get cheated since they cannot count the number of days worked, the number of bricks made or the number of bore-well pipes carried. Their monolingual existences make them perfect scapegoats for predatory labour contractors and middlemen. In a horrifying case documented by an NGO, 10 tribal youths of Ralegada Panchayat in Malkangiri district, Orissa had

---

[31] The Authors conversation with local NGOs in Andhra Pradesh- ASDS and Sitara in Bhadrachalem.

gone to Hyderabad to work as wage labourers for a bore-well company. In an accident one of the labourers lost a hand and was treated and sent back home. He was also given a compensation amount of Rs 10,000 by the company. In return the company forced the other nine labourers to work for six months to repay all the money spent on the injured labourer. The Government did nothing to provide justice to the labourers explaining that it was beyond their jurisdiction.

In another case, 24 tribals of Kartanpalli Panchayat in Malkangiri district had gone to Hyderabad as construction labourers. The labour contractor owed the labours Rs 24,000 each but sent them off without giving a single rupee. They did not have money for travel and so walked for one month to reach Kartanpalli. It was only because of a benevolent and proactive Collector who used a labour case to fine the contractor, that the dues to the labourers were paid. The middleman who took them to Hyderabad was also arrested and fined.

Thus alien places, unknown languages and unpolished skills make the life of migrants veritable hellholes. For the migrant tribals, forced out of his peaceful domain, it is a dual misery because while they lose their home and hearth to the conflict, they lose their livelihood and dignity with forced migration.

Finally, the only traditional source of livelihood still available to IDPs and tribals of conflict zone villages is NTFP marketing. Tribals continue to depend on weekly markets for their basic daily needs. Having lost their home and hearth and fearing to cultivate their land due to constant fear of ambush by police and Maoists, the tribals forage into the forests despite the fear of being suspected as Maoists. Whatever they are able to gather like medicinal fruits and leaves, edible roots and tubers, fuelwood, bamboo etc. they sell at accessible markets and buy rice, salt, oil and red chillies. It should be mentioned here that every tribal village accesses at least four local markets every week, but with the conflict raging even more intensely following the launch of Salwa Judum in 2005 and Operation Green Hunt in 2009, several rural weekly markets have been closed. This has been due to firing incidents wherein police personnel were killed by Maoists, due to fear of police and Maoists crossfire killing civilians and due to Salwa Judum camps coming up near these markets.

Closing down of the markets has impacted tribals in four basic ways – one, they are forced to walk for long distances to access markets, sometimes across the Andhra border. An example of this can be found in Chhattisgarh. Nelgoda village of Orchcha block used to depend on the Tumnar market, just 6 kms from the village but now tribals of Nelgoda have to go to Orchcha for the market which takes a total walk of 3 days up and down. Similarly, Lingagiri and villages around it used to access Basaguda, a market 2 kms from their village but had to walk two days up and down to Cherla in Andhra to access the market. However, Basaguda reopened in 2010. Similarly, Nendra villagers used to access Injaram market which is about 8 kms away but now have to walk two days up and down to Malaipenta in Andhra for marketing. In fact, Bheema Madkam, a tribal boy around 20 years old was arrested on his way back from Malaipenta in 2008 for allegedly carrying provisions for Maoists. In reality, Bheema was carrying 20 kgs rice from Malaipenta after selling *mahua* flowers there. It has been almost three years since he is in jail without any bail or magisterial hearings for his case. Nobody knows when Bheema, Sukhnath Oyami or Kopa Kunjam, tribals arrested under similar circumstances, will be acquitted and released from jail.

The closing down of markets also leads to great fear of being arrested. The men do not go to markets as they are under greater threat of being arrested hence it is mostly the women who go to the markets. For the tribals the weekly markets are not just places of economic exchange but places for social networking and tribal solidarity. This networking has totally broken down and communities are fragmented in almost irreparable ways. Thus, the breakdown of markets has led to a breakdown of socio-economic systems that bound the tribal society which is now falling apart.

Battered and Bruised - Women and Children under Assault

Women have borne the worst brunt in every conflict. Everywhere, in every conflict, women have become the victims of the wrath of the security forces and agencies like Salwa Judum and in instances of the Maoists. "In recent times, in land acquisition, in privatization of natural resources and water, in clearing the country to suit national and multinational capital, new laws have been introduced to suppress resistance, peaceful or otherwise. While this has wrecked havoc on the lives of lakhs of the most marginalized and destitute population of the country, it has had the greatest implications for women because of the presence of large number of paramilitary and military forces. In the past 25 years, in all incidences of mass rape by Assam Rifles in Manipur in the early 80s to Kupwara in Jammu and Kashmir, no justice has been accorded to the women and no punishment to the perpetrators. The brutal torture, gang-rape and killing of Manorama in July 2004 by Assam Rifles personnel in Manipur and the courageous protest of the Manipuri women against their continuous sexual abuse by armed forces, speaks volumes of the inhuman violence inflicted by the military and police on women in the name of counter-insurgency operations. Presently, driven by aggressive corporatisation, sustained state violence in Chhattisgarh, Jharkhand, Orissa and West Bengal and other states has become the single mantra to evict people from their land and livelihood. While this is being done in the name of 'development' or 'maintaining law and order', the real design is to appropriate resources and dispossess people of the area." This is what the activists of 'Women Against Sexual Violence and State Repression' (WSS), a national level body of women's rights activists and institutions, maintain in their statement of purpose. This very comprehensively puts the issue of violence, especially sexual violence, against women in a perspective.

K Balagopal, in his article, 'Physiognomy of Violence' says, "tribal women in Bastar in Chhattisgarh have been subjected to the most extreme forms of violence since 2005 by Salwa Judum, a civil militia created and funded by the state, to counter the Maoists. Villagers here have reported to local activists and NGOs, of incidents of gang rapes, custodial rape, mutilation of private parts, murder and continuous sexual abuse in villages, police stations and relief camps set up by the state government in the area. The extra-judicial murder in 2006 of a tribal for being a Maoist and the subsequent gang-rape of his wife in front of her child for several days inside a police station in Sarguja by police personnel including the SP is one such documented case. We are shocked that there are not even official records and FIRs of cases of sexual violence in Dantewada. Despite more than 90 sworn affidavits filed in cases pending before the Supreme Court, statements made before National Human Rights Commission (NHRC) and letters to Superintendent of Police, police in Bastar refuse to register cases of rape by Salwa Judum goons. Finally when six women dared to file private complaints and make their statements before a Magistrate in Konta, there is inexplicable and inordinate delay of months together in registering the cases. In the meanwhile these women and their entire villages are being threatened and intimidated by accused and other Salwa Judum leaders and SPOs that the entire village would be burnt down and villagers implicated in Naxalite cases – a threat which they know is not an exaggeration."[32]

It is pertinent to add here that in the Konta rape cases, as has been abbreviated by the media, the accused were identified by the tribal women victims and even arrest warrants were issued, but they were never executed due to a 'deliberate' mistake in the address, perhaps a wrong father's name or so. Despite the fact that the accused have been roaming around in the open regularly, addressing public meetings and rallies challenging the police to arrest them, the police say they are unable to trace the accused. Thus, it is obvious that the state is tacitly supporting the accused and using ridiculous pleas to evade arresting them. *"We do not get adequate leave to go home and so ...."* This was the answer a para-military commando of Special Operations Group (SOG) of Orissa narrated to a question on why security forces are known to rape women from poor and disadvantaged communities.

Another major way in which women and children are impacted by the conflict is the constant exposure to harassment at the hands of police forces and threat of kidnapping or execution by the Maoists. During our field work we have found that tribal women are wearier of illegal detention of the men in their families than kidnapping by Maoists. What is of importance is that when any male member is either detained, kidnapped or disappears then they start their search with the hope of recovering dead or mutilated bodies. The hope of life is almost a dead expression in the jungles of Orissa and

---

[32] K Balagopal, "Chhattisgarh: Physiognomy of Violence", Economic and Political Weekly 41 (22) (3 June), 2183-2186

Chhattisgarh. Wherever we have been we have invariably found a small gathering of desolate women squatting in front of police stations with fear and helplessness written all over their faces. On query, they would relate to us stories of illegal detention or disappearance in case of men and rape and disappearance in case of women. The usual charges range from providing food and shelter to Maoists to being Sangam members or village unarmed cadres of Maoists or armed cadres of Dalams. Most often the tribals are detained illegally and forwarded to court only if the family members raise a voice with the courts or in the media. Such is the case of Arti Majhi, a minor tribal girl of Jadingi village under Adaba police station in Gajapati district, Orissa who was picked up for being Maoist. She was then raped for four days at the police camp and illegally detained in February 2010. Though she related the entire case before the judge, no cognizance was taken of rape or illegal detention charges. Her father filed a case in the court but hearing on this is pending.

Due to regular combing operations in tribal villages by security forces, the villagers are constantly exposed to threats of arrests and assault. In a classic case, a tribal man of Paplur Panchayat in Malkangiri district of Orissa was picked up by the Greyhounds of Andhra police on 24th July 2010. While his wife and old father went from pillar to post looking for him at Vishakhapatnam, Koraput, Rayagada and Dantewada they could not find him anywhere. They appealed to the Superintendent of Police and other police officials but nobody gave them a hearing. Finally on 18th August 2010 he appeared in the village in an exhausted and extremely ill condition. He had been beaten and starved by the police. He related his story that the Greyhounds had picked him up from the village during a combing operation because he had a wound on his knee which the police insisted was from training at Maoist camps. Despite his denials he was detained and made to walk for about 200 kms over 3 days from Paplur to Vishakhapatnam where he was illegally detained in a police camp, then brought to Koraput and from there to Kalimela and finally let off at Bhejangwada police station.

Similarly, in another instance the Greyhounds arrested 11 tribals of Ralegada Panchayat of Malkangiri, of which four were women, at a weekly market in Andhra. They were taken to Vishakhapatnam and forwarded to court and brought out on bail by their Sarpanch after their villagers contributed around Rs 20,000. The worst fact is that of the four women, one was 7 months pregnant and another had an infant with her but they were not spared and tortured mentally and physically during the illegal detention. There is also the instance of Mangdu, who was arrested and acquitted for being a Maoist three years back. His past soon caught up and in the current Green Hunt offensive he was hunted down by the police. Anticipating illegal detention and arrest, Mangdu hid in the hills for about a month. In the meantime, the police harassed his wife and three daughters by entering their home at 4 am in the morning through the roof and threatened to take away their daughter if Mangdu did not surrender. It was after his wife went on regional media about this harassment that the Collector intervened and pursuit of Mangdu was dropped.

Very often women were intercepted by police to query on whereabouts of male kith and kin and ended up either arrested, assaulted or pursued by police. Unaware of disappearance of their family members, tribal women have no option left but to approach the police for information. These ordeals turn into nightmarish experiences that end in assault, rape or murder. The now media-abandoned case of rape of 8 Kandh tribal women of Vakapalli in Paderu division under Vishakhapatnam agency area of Andhra by Greyhounds is a case that reflects the dirt that war throws up. On 20th August 2007, 21 Greyhound police raided village Vakapalli looking for Maoists. Unable to find the men of the village who had fled to the forests, they raped 11 women. This brutal and terrible crime was brought to the notice of the police, government and judiciary and the media played a positive role by highlighting the case and followed it up. An enquiry was instituted and the women were made to go through a medical examination. While all evidences pointed to the guilt of the police personnel, the Government deliberately suppressed the medical examination and enquiry reports and soon it went out of public debate. Only a criminal case was registered but not a single accused has been arrested till date. Instead of supporting the truth the police have been threatening the women, the village men, local political representatives and lawyers involved in this case. There is allegation that some police officers of the rank of ASP have tried to buy off the women. In such cases and in all cases of sexual violence, justice delayed is definitely justice denied. This is no more an unusual reality for the tribals, especially the women.

In all, tribal women living in conflict zones are facing intensifying incidences of sexual violence with their fake encounter, denial of registering cases against the accused, threats to witnesses and illegal arrests or harassment. One positive outcome in the recent cases of violence against women is the relief given to the three widows of a fake encounter case inside Matwada camp way back in 2008. Police personnel, SPOs and Salwa Judum leaders had mercilessly thrashed and crushed to death three tribals in front of their wives in Matwada camp, Bijapur district, Chattisgarh. Initially the police refused to register any case against the accused, but after a lot of media highlight and a case in the local district court, a case was registered. The widows had to approach Chhattisgarh High Court when justice eluded them and finally the court ruled that the Government would pay compensation to the widows and take cognizance of the murders by police and institute cases against the accused for further prosecution.

If the above were instances of sexual and criminal offenses against women in conflict zones, then we will be doing injustice without mentioning economic violence. Having lost their home, village, land and forests to the conflict, the tribals live in a perpetual state of fear. Forced to have dual lives, tribal women keep their most basic household needs and food grains packed in sacs which can be carried into the forests during any emergency. Emergency here means a combing operation by the security forces, assault on the village by Salwa Judum mob or vengeful camping by Maoists in the village. This puts huge extra burden on managing the home front as men are constantly under watch by both the police and Maoists. The women manage two families, one in Chhattisgarh and one either in the forests of Chattisgarh or IDP settlements in Andhra. In other instances, the families send away the adolescent girls and male youths to IDP settlements and stay back in the village shuttling between the forest hut and village home.

It is pertinent to understand here that the tribal does not exist without the land and forests and so whatever the intensity of the conflict, they try their hardest to manage the conflict by finding unique but taxing ways of keeping their control on their land and forests. Such is their link that they take the pain of going back and forth between *mahua* season, agriculture season, harvesting season and the festival seasons, but do not manage the courage to stay put in Chhattisgarh the whole year through. The Government wants this control to be loosened and lost and therefore there is this whole repression in the name of Operation Green Hunt.

The whole burden of home making and management is solely on women – they gather food, keep the animals and go to the markets for selling and buying of provisions. This further exposes them to economic exploitation. While women are the ones who go to markets, even they do not go alone. Every village forms into women groups and go to the markets in these groups. But the non-tribal traders swoop down on the women like hawks and have found a crude way of getting the women to sell their forest products to them. They pick up the infants tagging along to the skirts or saris of the women. This forces the women to sell their products to the trader who grabbed the child and so there is no scope for bargain or alternate buyers.

Other Significant Fallouts

Shrinking Democratic Space

In addition to the most wretched condition that the tribals have been reduced to, this whole theatre of 'naxal threat' has had an adverse effect on the very soul of the country that makes any citizen take pride in – 'democracy'. India has claimed to be the greatest democracy in the world, thriving on principles of secularism and plurality in belief, thought and practice.

Today, never has the country witnessed such clamp down on civil society groups. The arrest of Binayak Sen, a medical doctor by profession and civil rights activist, the promulgation of public security acts to enable easy arrests of those who are perceived as threats merely as they openly criticize state actions, propping up pseudo-pro-state groups to publicly slander peace activists, academicians, women's rights workers, disallow press-meetings or public rallies etc. All these and many others are deliberate attempts to clamp down on the democratic space available and utilized by citizens to bring across their point of view.

Over Reacting-Under Reporting Media

The character of Media has, in any case, undergone drastic change since globalization, especially electronic media with each channel fighting for space and being the first to air 'dramatic news'. In situations such as these, the media almost sits as judges conducting public trials much before facts are unearthed, victims of abuse have been spoken to, opinion from perpetrators taken and judged. Print media except a few, especially national dailies are able to withstand the pressures of local administration, rest of them bring out press-releases from the state governments as news. In fact, local news media is pressurised against reporting or bringing out factual details, they are not allowed to report opposing views or carry press-reports of Community Party of India (Maoists). Some are even threatened with arrests.

Collapse of Governance – Heightened Corruption

Naxal threat has become synonymous to long-leaves by government functionaries such as school teachers, health personnel, ICDS workers and such others. The fear of being attacked has abandoned villages with no infrastructure. When there was an cholera outburst, basic help for life-saving was difficult. Over a 100 persons lost their lives. The threat perception that tribals feed naxals from their monthly collection under the food security scheme from public distribution shops (PDS) was enough to close down the PDS and have the quota sent to district head quarters forcing the villagers to walk for days to collect their quota. Surviving victims of abuse from security forces and police find it impossible to lodge complaints at police stations and there is complete collapse of the rule of law. In the midst of this, corrupt practices thrive stalling transfers by government functionaries to interior villages. In return for money utilization certificates of government work done is generated liberally. In heightened conflict districts such as Dantewada, Bijapur, Koraput, Malkangiri, it is most often the Superintendent of Police who has a free hand – 'the boss' – and not really the Collector.

Where do we go from Here?

As we write this chapter, people from the civil liberties groups, academia, tribal rights activists, bureaucrats, army personnel, political leaders are crying hoarse to pause and not engage in anything that will aggravate the situation for the tribals. These voices need to be heard along with the silent glares of the tribals. It is wisdom that needs to prevail not rage or anger.

Perhaps this is an opportunity, unfortunately with tragic loss of lives though, for the Indian State to re-examine its path of growth and development. Perhaps it is time to sit with tribal men, women and children and listen to what they have to say.

THE NAXAL INSURGENCY: CHALLENGES FOR THE PARAMILITARY FORCES

K S Sood

On 6 April 2010, the killing of 76 CRPF personnel in an ambush by Maoists in Dantewada stunned the nation and questioned the preparedness, motivation and training of the Indian Police and Central Paramilitary Forces (CPMFs). It also raised questions about the government's policy. The incident clearly showed that the security forces have become a target of the heightened violence in the 'Red Corridor'. Recurring attacks on security personnel and innocent civilians is indeed a challenge to India's democratic set up. In 2010, security forces suffered 226 casualties in counter-insurgency operations in the Left Wing Extremism (LWE) affected States. In 2009, 312 out of a total of 431 casualties were from the security forces and in 2008, more than 57% of the total casualties were reported from the LWE states. The government's response to the insurgency has been marred by a difference of opinion between its key officials. While some of them support a hard military response, others find this flawed and suggest a development approach. On the other hand the CPI (Maoists) has decided to take the government head on and make the best of the differences within the government. The contradictions within the government have confused the public and diluted an effective and determined policy approach against the Maoists.

Even after six decades of counter insurgency experience, we are still struggling in our efforts to contain naxal violence due to structural and systematic deficiencies. The government has relied on CPMFs to deal with insurgencies and other disorders as they are easily available and can be a rapidly deployed to tackle any crisis. However due to continuous expansion of the theatres of violence, CPMFs are under severe pressure and are unable to cope up with the situation. An analysis of the 'threat' dimension will reveal the role of the paramilitary forces, an analysis of the 'capability' dimension will reveal the structures, manpower and resources needed to achieve the organisational objectives; and an analysis of the 'time' dimension will reveal the urgency of creating the required paramilitary capability. Tremendous efforts are required on the capability dimension to deal with the insurgency in an effective and proactive way and to meet the existing and emerging challenges. The question is, are the troops in these areas, physically fit, well trained, mentally alert and logistically well-equipped to take on counter-insurgency operations in the tough terrains of LWE affected states?

The country's internal security situation demands a robust policing and paramilitary framework. Capabilities at Police Station level and in CPMFs at Platoon and Company level have to be adequate and must go hand in hand to meet the challenges. In the rapidly changing internal security scenario, the role assigned to CPMFs has undergone substantial changes. Para-military forces today are multi-task forces dealing with security, counter insurgency, law and order, border management, election duty and disaster management to list just a few.

In sub-conventional operations requirements are different from conventional operations. Sub-conventional operations are the most difficult because the concept of enemy cannot be applied to own people. As a result the role of CPMFs has become more challenging. Having served both in the Army and BSF I would not hesitate to note that life in Paramilitary forces is tough as everyday there are numerous challenges without any respite.

CPMFs have been expanding for the last 10-15 years and new battalions are being raised at break neck speed. However, proper training of the men and modernization of their equipment has not advanced at the same pace. In spite of expansion at a large scale the Paramilitary Forces face grave challenges and have no respite. Mere increase in the number of battalions will not enhance their efficiency when one views the weaknesses in command and control, organizational structure and the state of training. Some of the reasons for setbacks have been the lack of the Paramilitary forces to innovate at the tactical level, lack of vigor at the junior levels of command, and not learning from the past mistakes. The Dantewada tragedy in which 75 CRPF personnel were brutally killed in an ambush was a serious operational failure and shows the inability of the Police and Paramilitary Forces to contain the Naxal violence.

Despite simmering resentment within the rank and file, life goes on. A middle ranking CRPF officer said that, "those who understand the ground realities do not have the power to decide and those who have the power to decide do not understand the ground realities." We must draw lessons from the actions of operationally deployed Platoons and Companies which are the source of rich ground experience, instead of strategy being planned by inexperienced officers who have never served on the field, and unaware of ground realities.

On the other hand the militarization and lethal capabilities of Naxals are on the rise. Naxalites have attacked Paramilitary camps and fought pitched battles for hours. They have well-coordinated, trained and ideologically brainwashed cadres and units. LWE tactic involves luring the forces into a trap. Armed Naxal cadres who have no fear of the presence of security forces can now gather in Battalion (Bn) / Brigade size groups at their time and place of choice. CPMFs have the obvious disadvantage of not knowing the local language, area, customs, traditions and it is here that the role of well trained local Police comes to play.

State Police

Police is a strong arm of the Government, its strength and efficiency is essential for the Government's credibility. Civil police have roots in the society, they belong to that area, have deep knowledge of the terrain, know the local language and have bonds with the people. This network and knowledge is the key to success in any counter insurgency operation. Punjab and Andhra Pradesh provide an outstanding example of success achieved by the local police and Paramilitary forces in counterinsurgency campaigns. No counterinsurgency campaign can succeed without the cooperation of the local police. After analyzing a series of Naxal incidents, the grey areas in police training can be summarized as follows:-

a) Lack of physical and mental robustness.

b) Lack of soldierly and disciplinary traits.

c) Lack of knowledge of field craft and tactics.

d) Poor firing skills.

A well trained, professionally committed and motivated local police force along with CPMFs can tackle any type of internal disorder. However, at present there is a mismatch in training capabilities and infrastructure in most of the States. Nevertheless the Special Task Force (STF) personnel in most of the Naxalism- affected States are generally performing better as they are better trained. They only need to completely switch over to the combat role. Paramilitary forces can achieve outstanding results against the insurgents only when they work in close coordination with the local police forces. But Paramilitary forces at times, feel hesitant in having close liaison with the Police and do not feel comfortable in taking orders or working under the directions of local Police.

Modernization of Police and Paramilitary forces should go hand in hand as their duties are complimentary in counter insurgency operations. This should be done to strengthen the Police at the police station level instead of a top- down approach. In order to enhance the capabilities of Police and Paramilitary Forces in Naxal affected States, the Centre and State Government have to take numerous steps. These steps include improving the combat capability of Special Police Forces (SPFs) by establishing special anti-Naxal forces, specialized training to SPFs in counter insurgency and jungle warfare, providing better arms, ammunition, equipment and BP vehicles.

Challenges

We need to examine as to why different organizations with same weapons and manpower and from the same background perform differently in anti-terrorist and anti-insurgency operations. Difference in performance is due to lack of leadership, chain of command, neglect of training, higher age profile, professional ethos, manner of employment, regimentation, and logistics and its responsiveness.

BSF and CRPF are the main Paramilitary forces fighting terrorism, insurgency and naxalism. BSF that was raised in 1965 with 25 Bns now has 159 Bns. Each Bn has seven Companies with a strength of 137 personnel each. However, the effective strength of a company when it moves out to an operational area is only 75 to 80 personnel and if the Company is deployed in any operational area it will have a fighting strength of only 60-65 after catering for administration and other duties.

British raised Crown Representative Police in 1939 to quell "dacoity" in States. After Independence it became Central Reserve Police. It was deployed on Indo-China and Indo-Pak borders along with the Army. In 1974 it became CRPF with the basic role of providing reserve assistance to States/UTs in police operations to maintain law and order and to contain insurgency. Despite the term 'Force', it still has the word 'Police' and is treated as Police. It has various roles – crowd control, election duty, law and order problem, counter insurgency, personnel security, protection of flora and fauna etc. CRPF has 208 Bns and is the biggest Paramilitary force in the world.

Why are CPMFs not able to meet the challenges that face them. The answers lie in the following factors:-

a) Organizational structure at Functional level needs a change.

b) Inadequacy in training imparted to Police and CPMFs.

c) Lack of coordination between Police and CPMFs.

d) Non availability of reserves.

e) Lack of effective leadership.

f) Lack of actionable Intelligence.

g) Prolonged deployments.

h) Lack of regimentation.

j) Low morale and motivation.

k) Political interference in working of Police and CPMFS.

Organizational Structure at Functional Level Needs a Change

Paramilitary forces should work on doctrines based on latest strategic perceptions and by structuring the organization accordingly. Internal Security duties demand a manpower intensive establishment at the activity level i.e. at the Platoon and Company level. In a Company the effective strength is 75–80 out of 137 personnel. Such seven Companies with small functional strength can affect the operational capability of a Battalion. Therefore the number of Companies should be reduced to four, but at the same time there should be an increase in the strength of the Company from 137 to 190 so that a minimum 150 men are available in each Company for the operations. A weak Platoon or Company in terms of manpower does not instill confidence in a junior commander. Therefore changes at the basic structural level are the need of the hour.

Inadequacy in Training imparted to Police and CPMFs

The fact that a sub unit of a well organized Paramilitary force was literally massacred raises some serious questions on the training and adherence to basic tactics/field craft. Case studies of Naxal related incidents have revealed that one of the prime reasons for recurring security force casualties has been the inadequacy in training imparted to them. Training has to be realistic, dynamic, progressive and responsive to the changing environment. To remain responsive to emerging challenges, the curriculum both conceptually and contextually should be reviewed periodically. However there is no such Directorate in CPMFs which can function as a think-tank and generate ideas, concepts and eventually a doctrine responsive to the present day training needs.

With the passage of time and multifarious commitments, the culture of training has eroded in CPMFs. Senior commanders are unable to implement training programmes due to heavy commitments of the CPMFs in multifarious administrative and security duties. After 1988 hardly any collective training has been carried out at Bn/Coy level in CPMFs due to heavy commitments. Most of the training pamphlets have also not been revised during the last 15 years.

Is it reasonable to expect a person trained like a policeman to perform like a commando after six/eight weeks of pre-induction training? What about his mindset and reflexes? Can you change the mind set and reflexes of a 50 year old person in six weeks?

CRPF has got five Recruit Training Centers, each capable of training 1200 recruits in a year. 69 CRPF Battalions have been raised during the last ten years mostly at Group Centers instead of Recruit Training Centers, without proper trainers, ranges, equipment and accommodation. CRPFs prestigious training centre at Neemuch has a Recruit Training Centre and Central Training College which conducts approximately 48 Courses in a year. Only eight officers are authorized as instructors and they perform other duties also. In the Army, for example to run a single Junior Command course 1 Major General, 5 Brigadiers and 48 Colonels are available. So you can imagine their standard of training, flawlessness, and professional soundness.

In the absence of an effective evaluation system to monitor the training imparted, no one is accountable for the final outcome. The focus at times shifts to maintenance of the area, parks, and officer's mess, places that a VIP is likely to visit and appreciate. There is tremendous pressure on the availability of training areas and firing ranges due to rapid urbanization. Therefore we need to improve our training infrastructure. There are 215 State Police and 69 Central Training Institutes in the country. A large number of State Police training Institutes do not have a proper team of Instructors. In State police, posting in a Police training centre is considered as a punishment posting and such type of unwilling personnel cannot impart training in a real sense.

A survey revealed the following:-

- Very few training institutions have published training material for use by the trainees.

- Quality of trainers is generally poor and posting in a police training centre is considered as a punishment posting.

- 23 Police training institutions were functioning without classrooms, 18 without blackboards, 16 without overhead projectors, 57 without conference rooms, 76 without seminar or assembly halls, 20 without library, 70 without auditorium, 93 without simulation facilities and 72 without computers.

Cobra Bns now called SAF (Special Action Force) Battalions of CRPF are doing a much better job in anti Naxal operations because they are a younger lot, better trained and highly motivated. Each SAF Battalion has 33 young officers compared to 14 officers in a regular Battalion. We certainly need more SAF Battalions to take on the Naxalites.

There is a need, for certain amount of structured training at training centers for Counter insurgency apart from re-orientation training before their deployment. Well trained CPMFs are in the national interest, as they are of great help to the Army in a hot war scenario.

Lack of Coordination between Police and CPMFs

Lack of coordination between State and CPMF became public in July 2010, when Chhattisgarh DGP, said, "We can't teach the CRPF how to walk," after the Centre called for "relocation and reconfiguration" of CPMF. Special DG (Naxal Operations) CRPF retaliated with an allegation of non-cooperation from state police. The problem of coordination persists at various levels thus hampering the performance of Paramilitary Forces. Most of the times it becomes an ego based issue.

Lack of coordination is also evident in the lack of understanding of operational ethos and gap in training. Police personnel train separately but work jointly with CPMFs in counter insurgency operations, which is a major handicap in ensuring coordination at all levels. The training of State police and Paramilitary forces is totally different. Just as the newly raised India Reserve Battalions from some States are being sent to Border Security Force training centers for training, the State Armed Police and District Police personnel should also be sent for training to CPMFs. It is clear that something is amiss as far as the coordination is concerned at joint operational level.

After the Dantewada incident of 6th April 2010, CRPF is caught in a bureaucratic red tape as junior leadership has to take permission from its

HQs at New Delhi to launch any operation even on information given by the local police. By the time permission is received by the field commanders the Maoists move out.

Non Availability of Reserves

In Naxal areas deployment and operations are company based and a company covers an approximately vast area of 18-20 Kms. There are no reserves / reinforcements available in case of any eventuality. Some CPMF officers deployed in Orissa showed serious concern about the non availability of reinforcements / reserves to come to their rescue. This issue hovers in their minds and thus affects their performance and is manifest in their hesitation to venture out of their camps in an unknown terrain which is mined.

Lack of Effective Leadership

In counter insurgency operations where the stakes are very high, well trained and experienced officers, confer a sense of protection on their subordinates by virtue of their skills. In this harsh, dangerous and stressful environment, it is the effective leadership which will keep the high motivational levels.

The organizational process of identifying gaps in performance is important, and has to be an ongoing exercise. When the senior leadership has rarely stayed in tents or moved in jungles, it could be difficult to inspire cutting edge levels of command. The lessons have to be learnt, from the junior officers in the field who are engaged in actual combat.

Counter Insurgency operation is a small commander's war, fought at Company / Platoon level. Effective Counter Insurgency operations cannot be controlled by centralized command. This requires having faith in the junior leadership and allowing them to take decisions as they are the better judge of the ground realities. They should be made more accountable and responsible in handling the situations.

Lack of Actionable Intelligence

There are a large number of state and central intelligence agencies working in India but with little co-ordination amongst them. These agencies mainly work in urban and strategic areas, leaving vast rural areas uncovered.

Collection, collation and dissemination of information take a long time. When the Paramilitary forces move in they feel handicapped due to non availability of actionable intelligence. It is also not easy to gather information about the Naxalites in these areas, as Naxals have a terrorizing influence over the locals.

Naxalites use traditional methods of communication which the security forces find difficult to decipher. Locals living in the interior areas avoid the Police and would not dare to provide any information to the Police because of the fear to their lives from the Naxalites. The Paramilitary forces also find themselves handicapped as the Maoists are not using modern means of communications to avoid chances of detection and neutralization. Therefore there is no flow of technical intelligence.

Security Forces thus are more dependent on Human Intelligence, which is not forth coming. Urban sources do not hesitate, in reporting to the Police but in the case of Maoist insurgency, the villagers are reluctant to report against their co-villagers. Villages are thinly-populated in deep jungles, so Police informers get easily exposed where advantage of anonymity is weak and there is no protection for village sources against the backlash by the Maoists. The ability of the rural Police to collect information depends upon on its movement in the affected areas and its relationship with the village community. Fears caused by the frequent use of landmines and ambushes with devastating effects have hampered the movement and patrolling of the Police and CPMFs in rural areas and as a result there is a serious lack of police-community relationship. The Police and CPMFs are unable to remain in regular touch with the villagers and cannot collect worthwhile intelligence about the Naxalites.

BSF and CRPF have intelligence branches as an integral part of each Coy/Bn, but they are unable to mingle with local tribes due to language problems, unfamiliar area and due to the fact that they can be detected very easily. Lack of information is threfore a big challenge to launch INT based anti-Naxal operations.

Prolonged Deployments

Paramilitary forces especially CRPF personnel are deployed continuously on operational duties. There are very few static establishments, which accommodate less than 15% of the strength of CRPF personnel. This continuous deployment from one theatre to another exhausts them physically, mentally and psychologically and erodes their capabilities. You cannot expect good results from depressed personnel who most of the times live in inhuman conditions without proper accommodation in some States.

"In the Army field tenure is followed by a peace / hard peace posting in rotation. In peace posting they train hard. We, on the other hand, find ourselves in combat postings for a long time," said a CRPF official. In CPMFs there is no such opportunity when the troops are free. From border duties they move to election duty, law and order duty and counter insurgency duties. Therefore there is no respite for them.

In 2009, 14,422 Paramilitary Jawans applied for voluntary retirement from service which is an 85 percent increase from the previous year and 112 percent from 2007. On the other hand, only 4,622 soldiers sought voluntary retirement from the Indian Army, which is much bigger, than all the paramilitary forces put together.

Lack of Regimentation

Paramilitary forces have no regimentation hence no sense of belonging. For example in the Army a recruit retires from the same unit he joined upon being recruited. For a young officer there is no bigger honor than to command the unit in which he was commissioned. There have been numerous examples when an officer on promotion as a Commanding Officer opted to defer his promotion and wait for the present incumbent to finish his tenure, so that he can command the same unit which he joined on commission.

A soldier will sacrifice his life for the honor of his unit and not for the country. In response to a question "What makes them risk their life?" 82% responded in favour of Units pride. Regimentation is an essential ingredient of morale and motivation. This system should be adopted by CPMFs. The BSF has already begun such a practice.

Morale and Motivation

CPI (Maoists) have been able to induce fear in the minds of CPMFs by successful attacks and this coupled with inadequate training and equipment has adversely affected the morale of the troops.

CRPF attached to police stations is mainly deployed on Company/ Platoon base. CPMF units must operate as a cohesive Unit, under the direct command of the commanding officer and not as independent companies, with the commanding officer responsible only for administration. A commanding officer sitting in his Battalion HQ in Chennai cannot exercise effective operational control over his companies deployed for anti-Maoist operations in Chhattisgarh, Jharkhand and Andhra Pradesh. He cannot ensure high standards of training and morale of his men under his command while being miles away from those deployed miles away. It is ironical that even in such situations Commanding Officers are still held responsible for any operational or administrative lapse.

The ever increasing requirement of Paramilitary forces in counter insurgency operations from one theatre to another has become a regular feature, resulting in their constant and prolonged deployments in inhospitable terrain and aloof from their families. Low intensity conflict operations and proxy wars have put tremendous professional and psychological pressures on Para-military Forces. Counter insurgency operations are very tough but there is no rest and recreation for the troops.

A jawan joining BSF waits for approx 18 years to get his first promotion as a Head Constable. Rank of Lance Naik and Naik were done away with by the 5th Pay Commission on the recommendations of BSF. Hence to wait for 18 years to get first promotion has adversely affected the morale of the troops. BSF has now taken up a case for reintroduction of rank of Lance Naik and Naik.

Therefore, the importance of sustaining the motivation level and morale of troops in these circumstances, assumes added significance. Troops are facing stress, tension, frustration and anger which have resulted in low performance and large number of suicide cases. Numerical superiority of manpower or weapons does not motivate a jawan but highly motivated leadership can bring the desired results.

Higher Age Profile on CPMFs

Personnel in CPMFs from class IV to commandant retire at the age of 57 and those from the DIG rank and above retire at 60. The local promote officers are well past their middle age and cannot lead by example from front. Even lower ranks are in a higher age group and to expect these men to trek 15 Kms a day or move in jungles in humid conditions is asking for too much. CRPF which has 208 battalions can plan and bifurcate 100 battalions of personnel in the higher age group for exclusively tackling law and order problems and the remaining 108 battalions into a younger lot to be deployed for counter insurgency operations.

Political Interference in Working of Police and CPMFs

There is lot of interference in the working of Police by the leaders of political parties, especially those who are in power. For example, in Bihar the Special Auxiliary Police (SAP) with 4000 ex-army men was raised on a two-year contract, to fight Naxal outfits. The SAP succeeded in some cases and pushed the Naxalites back in spite of suffering some casualties. Today most of this elite force is now being utilized in providing protection to the VIPs of Bihar. Political leadership in some of the States is reluctant to join the war on Red Terror to remain in power. In some States Maoists are considered as a misled lot who should be dealt with sympathy and not by CPMFs. They have forgotten that the one point agenda of the Maoists is armed over throw of the Indian State and end of democracy in this country.

Conclusion

Maoist terrorism is the gravest threat to national security today. There is no unanimous stand in UPA on how to fight the Maoists. Union Home Minister seems to have washed of his hands of the matter after he was given a limited mandate for the use of Armed Forces to fight against the Maoists. The Congress allies in UPA are playing a double role. Mamta Banerjee openly condemned the killing of Maoist leader Azad in a so called Police encounter. Bihar Chief Minister has rejected the Union Government's proposal for joint operations against Maoists in Bihar. Unless and until political leadership is determined to deal sternly with Maoists, State Police and CPMFs cannot succeed.

Following a large number of serious set backs suffered at the hands of Maoists and in the absence of clear directions at the political level in different States the morale of the Police and CPMFs is low. There is an urgent need for upgrading the state police force in terms of transformation in doctrine, manpower utilization, training and methods through which they would operate in these areas. Military operations are the only dimension of the totality of strategies that the State needs to employ in such a serious internal conflict to save the country from disintegration.

CONTRIBUTORS

Ms. Tejal Chandan is a doctoral candidate at the Centre for International Politics, Organisation and Disarmament, School of International Studies, JNU, New Delhi. She has been research fellow with the Centre for Security Analysis, Chennai and has also worked with the United Nations University, Peace and Governance Programme in Tokyo, Japan. She held the National Security Fellowship offered by the US State Department's Institute of U.S. National Security at IGCC, University of California, San Diego in 2008 and is an alumnus of the Regional Centre for Strategic Studies Summer Workshop on Defence, Technology and Cooperative Security in South Asia. Her publications cover the issues of conflict resolution and peace building, national security, civil-military relations as well as civil society. She holds a Masters Degree in International Studies from the Department of Peace and Conflict Research at the Uppsala University in Sweden.

Ms Ancy Joseph is research assistant at the Centre for Security Analysis, Chennai. She has written articles on the conflict and the current affairs of Myanmar as well as on internal conflicts in South Asia. As a Research Assistant at CSA, she assists the Executive Director in carrying out the Center's programmes and projects. She holds a Master of Philosophy Degree in Public Administration and Masters Degrees in International Studies and Public Administration from the University of Madras. She also holds a Post Graduate Diploma in Business Administration from the Technical Education Department, Government of Kerala.

Dr. Sudha Ramachandran is an independent researcher/journalist based in Bangalore. She writes on South Asian politics and security issues. She was Assistant Editor at Deccan Herald (Bangalore) for five years. Dr Ramachandran has been freelancing since 2001 and contributes articles regularly to publications like Asia Times Online. She has reported from

Kashmir, Sri Lanka, Fiji and Northern Ireland, as well as on India's Maoists. She is a visiting lecturer at the Asian College of Journalism, Chennai and at Kulturstudier's (Oslo) Peace and Conflict program at Puducherry. She holds a doctoral degree from Jawaharlal Nehru University, New Delhi.

Dr. P.V. Ramana is a research fellow at the Institute for Defence Studies and Analyses (IDSA), New Delhi. His area of interest is South Asian Security Studies. Since 2002, Dr Ramana has been involved in studying the Naxalite-Maoist movements in India and the other South Asian countries. He has conducted extensive field work in Naxal affected states in India. He has contributed over 80 pieces on the Naxalite movement in India including chapters in books, research papers, articles in leading newspapers of India. He has published papers on Naxalism in many International journals like Defence and Security Analysis and Jane's Intelligence Review. Dr Ramana is on the guest faculty of the CRPF's Internal Security Academy, ITBP Academy, and Border Security Force Academy. He also delivers lectures annually for IFS probationers and senior IPS officers, as part of the training activities of IDSA. He was consulted by the All India Congress Committee (AICC)-appointed Task Force on Naxalite Violence, in 2005, in the preparation of its report.

Mr. E.N. Rammohan IPS (Retd) is former Director General of Border Security Force. Post retirement, he was Adviser to the Governor of Manipur. Recently, he conducted the one man enquiry to probe the massacre of the CRPF personnel by the Naxalites at Dantewada, Chhattisgarh.

Ms. Sharanya Nayak is associated with Action Aid for the past twelve years. Having closely worked with the tribal communities in the southern part of Chhattisgarh and Orissa, she has developed in-depth understanding of the socio-political, cultural and economic structure of these tribal groups. She was a sub-editor of the New Indian Express for two years. She is a postgraduate in Sociology.

Ms. Malini Subramaniam is an independent social researcher from Raipur, Chhattisgarh. She has worked with Action Aid, India in various capacities and was also associated with Oxfam. She has taken up short term research assignments with Institute of Development Studies, Sussex United

Kingdom, UNICEF, Japan International Cooperation (JICA). She holds a postgraduate degree in Social Work from Tata Institute of Social Sciences, Mumbai. Her areas of interest are gender and child issues.

Mr. K.S. Sood served in the Indian Army as a Commissioned Officer and later joined Border Security Force in 1975 and retired in 2007. He has served in Assam, Tripura, Mizoram, Rajasthan, J&K, Gujarat and Punjab. He has vast field experience including counter-insurgency operations, internal security, intelligence gathering and border management. He has been decorated with "Police Medal for Gallantry", "Police Medal for Meritorious Service" and three times recipient of "Director General BSF Commendation Roll" for praise worthy performance in operations and training. As an Instructor, he was Commander of Tactical Wing and Commando School of Border Security Force Academy and has made substantial contributions in the training of officers.

CSA PUBLICATIONS

CONFLICT RESOLUTION AND PEACE BUILDING

1.   Conflict Resolution and Peace Building in Sri Lanka

2.   Federalism and Conflict Resolution in Sri Lanka

3.   Peace Process in Sri Lanka: Challenges & Opportunities

4.   Conflict Over Fisheries in the Palk Bay Region

5.   Conflict in Sri Lanka: The Road Ahead

6.   Peace and Conflict Resolution: Emerging Ideas

7.   From Winning the War to Winning Peace: Post War Rebuilding of the Society in Sri Lanka

8.   Internal Conflicts in Myanmar: Transnational Consequences

9.   Internal Conflict in Nepal: Transnational Consequences

SECURITY STUDIES

10. US and the Rising Powers: India and China

11. Maritime Security in the Indian Ocean Region: Critical Issues in Debate

12. Public Perceptions of Security in India: Results of a National Survey

13. Essential Components of National Security

CIVIL SOCIETY AND GOVERNANCE

www.ingramcontent.com/pod-product-compliance
Lightning Source LLC
Chambersburg PA
CBHW070810300326
41914CB00078B/1926/J